Cricut for Beginners

All-in-One Book: Design Space + Project Ideas + Accessories + Materials + How to Make Money With a Cricut Machine. Simple Step-by-Step Guide to Get You Mastering All the Potentials of Your Machine. Detailed Practical Examples Included

Annabelle J. Maker

contained within this document, including, but not limited to, errors, omissions, or inaccuracies.

Table of Contents

Introduction

Do you want to create homemade accessories, office supplies, jewelry, and prints? Do you also wish to make valuable craftwork from the comfort of your home? If so, *Cricut For Beginners: All-in-One Book: Design Space + Project Ideas + Accessories + Materials + How to Make Money With a Cricut Machine. Simple Step-by-Step Guide to Get You Mastering All the Potentials of Your Machine* is the place to get your answers!

This book will teach you everything you need to know about Cricut die-cutters (including the Cricut Maker, the Explore Air 2, and the Cricut Joy). It will also teach you about Cricut Design Space software for creating unique images, drawings, and prints, and give you 10+ profitable creative projects from beginner levels to advanced.

After reading through the book, you will have gained all the knowledge and skills necessary for successful and profitable Cricut creations. You will first learn the Cricut basics, including how the machine works. After all, cutting, drawing, and writing with Cricut will require understanding how the machine functions, how its parts operate, and, of course, how to work in its app, called "Design Space".

Once you know what die-cutting truly is and isn't, as well as the type of products you can (and cannot) create with it, you'll have a good idea about the type of materials you want to work with, the products you wish to make, and the type of the machine you want.

Keep in mind that in order to get the most out of your Cricut machine(s), you'll need to decide which is the best model to get. This book will review Cricut's three most popular machines: Cricut Maker, Explore Air 2, and Cricut Joy. Throughout the journey, we will go over dimensions, operations, capacities, and the types of craftwork each of the machines is capable of making. We will discuss expenses as well so that you can decide which of the models is the best choice for you.

By the time you're finished, you might decide that you're good with the simple Cricut Joy, or you may wish to go big from the start and order a full Cricut Maker, including all of the add-ons and materials. This book will go over the machine's different features so that you can figure out which of them meets your needs.

After gaining knowledge concerning how Cricut machines work, you'll need to learn how to operate them on your own. For this reason, this book will take you step by step through Cricut creation. First, you'll learn how to set up the machine, connect it to your device, and use Design Space. As you will soon find out, Design Space is the place where you'll create your unique designs. This book will be your thorough guide through the app's structure, tabs, options, functions, and operations. It will show you the exact pathways you need to take to draw, layer, edit, and erase images and fonts.

This book will show you how to use the app for proper cutting, drawing, folding, embossing, and other complex functions. This won't be yet another inspiring tutorial that turns out to be impossible to apply; this book will give you exact pathways for each of the main operations, as well as tips and tricks for creating the most beautiful, top-quality results!

Once you're familiar with the right techniques for Cricut craftwork, you will learn how to use the machine correctly, clean it, and set it up so that it functions seamlessly. This will extend its lifespan and ensure that you're using it correctly, which will keep it working longer. You'll receive a detailed guide for how to attach and detach different add-ons and machine parts, as well as how to maintain them to prevent damage to its materials.

So, in other words, this book will provide you with *all* the details you need to know, including how to store, clean, and lubricate your machine's blade, and even which clothes and cleaners to use. It is a comprehensive guide to get you started, keep you going, and achieve expert status on the Cricut machine.

Are you in? Then let's begin!

Chapter 1:

Cricut Basics: What Is Cricut and

Why Do You Need It?

If you picked up this book, you most likely know that a Cricut machine can help make all sorts of useful shapes for your artwork or hobby. But what exactly does this machine do and how does it work?

If you decided to purchase one of these neat tools, you were probably drawn by the possibility of being able to streamline the cutting of different shapes on a variety of materials. You might imagine using Cricut to easily make a piece of clothing, a decoration, fun refrigerator magnets, stickers, or even an ornamental mini-shelf for your living room. Perhaps you're wondering if all these things are possible to do with Cricut, and if so, what type of machine will you need and how much will the work cost. Keep reading to find out the answers to these questions (and so much more!).

6

What Is a Cricut Machine?

A Cricut machine is a device that can help you streamline your cutting of different types of materials. This is useful if you don't have enough time, skill, or precision to do your own manual cutting. You can use it to make ornaments, shirts, or all kinds of useful stickers with laser precision and accuracy (Sund, 2010).

Cricut is a brand that features multiple products. They carry embossers and heat presses, but more importantly, they feature die-cutting machines that ended up becoming a household name. A Cricut machine is a die-cutting apparatus that you can use at home for your creative projects, artwork, and crafts. However, there is a twist with these machines that makes them unique and highly convenient. They are smart machines that can cut all sorts of shapes out of paper, vinyl, thin plates of cardboard, all sorts of MDF (medium-density fibreboard), wood, and other materials.

Moreover, the latest versions of Cricut machines can also draw with pens, and they can score your paper or cardboard for easy and precise folding (think next-level—intricate yet effortless origami artwork, for example).

The Cricut name alone refers to the brand, but the popularity of their die-cutting machines made its use synonymous with these specific cutters. While the limits to the utilization of Cricut cutters solely depend on your imagination, the mechanics behind how they operate are a different issue. The proper use of Cricut machines requires an understanding of how they work, as well as how they should be used to get the best value for your investment.

How Do Cricut Die-Cutting Machines Work?

Cricut machine cutters operate simply and conveniently. First, you need to create a design, which needs to be in an image form, on your computer. After this, you need to send your shape to the cutting machine via a Bluetooth connection or a USB cable.

After the machine receives the right shape to be cut, it then operates its computer which navigates a cutting blade. The principle is similar to how a printer works with its ink nozzle, but here, the machine's computer guides the plate to cut an exact copy of the shape that you created on your computer.

Aside from cutting, the newest Cricut models can emboss, engrave, score, and write using the same principle. This means that working with a Cricut machine covers three main operations:

- Creating your design
- Sending it to the machine and telling it what to do (cut, write, engrave, etc.)
- Doing the hard work while you sit back and sip on your coffee

https://pixabay.com/illustrations/home-at-home-decoration-wood-2194174/

Your Cricut machine will come with a couple of add-ons, like different cutter models, cords, instructions, a cutting mat, and more. You will also receive a USB cable and a power adapter, and even one or two dozen projects that you can start making as soon as you plug in your machine. Depending on the model you choose, you can get a special writing pen and scoring wheels as well.

As you can see, the Cricut die-cutting machine isn't a simple cutter. For example, let's say you want to make your own wedding invitations. A Cricut lets you design the layout and text, size, and shape right on your computer. After that, all you need to do is get the correct type of paper ready, insert it into the machine, and let it cut out the card shapes, draw on the text, and score your wedding invitations for folding if needed. Neat, right?

No longer will you need to make an order, then wait to see if your invitations turned out well nor will you have to send the cards back if the writing is wrong. The machine also results in much lower expenses, and arguably, much more convenience since you are creating just the type of card you envisioned.

The trick with using Cricut machines is that you'll have to learn how to work with each model's specific brand software, which is free to download. This book will help you do that as well, so relax and enjoy the read!

Aside from the brand's software, you can also use other apps that are compatible with the machine, but this book will focus on creating designs and images from scratch on the brand's app.

What Can You Make With a Cricut Machine?

https://pixabay.com/photos/daisy-heart-thank-you-love-2313940/

Now, we come to the truly fun part of working with a Cricut machine. When being creative with a Cricut, your only limitations stem from the type of materials the machine can handle and its installed features. Other than that, the shapes you'll create and the purpose they'll serve are left to your imagination.

Various types of these cutters will be covered in the next chapter, as they have slightly different features and potentials. For now, though, we will go over some of the amazing things you can create with a Cricut.

- **Scrapbooking and decorations.** If you want to make an amazing vision board, a scrapbook, or an inspirational poster, a Cricut is a neat tool to have since finished products like these can cost quite a bit. A Cricut lets you print and cut shapes, words, letters, or even entire sentences and quotes. With this in mind, you can use it for a cleverly designed organization panel or a vision board, to cut out meaningful quotes and add them to your journal, scrapbook, or hang on a wall, and so much more.

- **Cards and envelopes.** Whether it's a gift card, a letter, or an event invitation, the average Cricut has built-in operations that can either streamline the cutting and folding of shapes or incorporate beautiful prints and embossment for a finer look. Having this possibility in your own home can make your life a lot easier. From not having to run and buy envelopes, to being able to make personalized invitations for your child's birthday or even creating luxury greeting cards and business cards—the possibilities are endless with a Cricut machine. Plus, printing and sending family pictures to make holiday cards will save you major bucks. Ordering personalized products such as these can cost hundreds of dollars, but printing and cutting with your machine costs next to nothing. All you need to do is grab your chosen type of paper, and you're good to go.

- **Home and accessories.** Cricuts can cut through smaller pieces of fabric, and you can use them to make easy baby onesies, leggings, and shirts. All you need to do is either create or download a pattern, let the machine do its work, and then sew in the pieces of fabric knowing that they'll be just the right design and fit. The same principle can be used when making or repurposing linens, mats, or wall decals. Imagine being able to repurpose a worn-out T-shirt into a small pillowcase or a fine towel. Cool, right? Cricut machines also give you the possibility to make your own window decals, organization labels, banners, and buntings.

- **Interior design.** Aside from being able to cut unique decorations, a Cricut is also ideal for making your own painting stencils, picture frames, and quote artwork. You can also use it to make a matching pillow, sofa cushions, and other creations. With the help of a Cricut machine, you have the ability to effortlessly cut Christmas ornaments, party decorations, and even prints for glasses and mugs.

- **Jewelry.** If you learn how to work with a Cricut die-cutter, you can also make your custom jewelry, like leather bracelets, custom earrings, pendants, and so much more! You can also make a custom pet collar, and do countless other DIY projects!
- **Business and office.** A Cricut allows you to make your very own personalized, brand calendars, stickers, bullet journals, planner designs, and business cards. If you own a business or you're planning to start one, you can use a Cricut to put your brand name, logo, and business information on all sorts of promotional products, like keychains, mugs, coasters, and other items.

What Can't You Do or Make With a Cricut Machine?

Your projects will depend on the specific possibilities of the Cricut model you choose. That being said, there are a couple of general limitations that apply to all Cricuts:

- **Printing.** Your Cricut won't be able to print images. However, you can use it for pen writing and apply numerous types of pens and ink for drawing. This gives you the possibility to choose text, colors, font, and size for any writing you wish to put on paper, even though you cannot print exact images. Instead, you'll have to provide a layout with the chosen color, pattern, or image to cut in the desired shape and apply the writing. This entails some careful thinking when making your designs. Keeping in mind that any images you wish to include are going to have to be printed in advance, you can later cut them using a Cricut. This way, you can apply a chosen image or pattern in the form of a sticker or transfer it onto the material before you start cutting more shapes and writing.

- **Sewing and gluing**. Your Cricut can produce pieces for your project and decorate them with the type of writing you choose if you pick a more advanced model. However, your project will require further planning when it comes to putting a piece of work together. This might sound mundane at first, but you can easily find yourself lacking tools, supplies, or time to finish a project if you rely on the machine too much.

- **Safety**. Depending on the intended purpose of your project, all safety concerns are going to have to be thought through in advance. The safety and endurance of your finished piece will have to be accounted for when thinking about the size and shape of your design, as it strongly depends on the safety and sturdiness of the materials you use. For example, if you wish to cut out children's toys, you'll have to make sure that your design doesn't feature shapes that can be easily broken off or swallowed or that are too sharp and pointy. Likewise, it is up to you to ensure that the materials you use are suitable for the intended purpose of the final product. It might sound appealing to use a Cricut for home decorations or even cutlery, but equal attention is necessary when choosing the most suitable and safest materials that will endure the strain that will be put on the object you plan to create.

- **Quality**. Similar to safety, the quality and the life span of your work will depend on your choice of materials. Decorative pieces might not require particular material pickiness, but if the objects you're making are going to have to be washed, folded, or handled frequently, you'd be wise to look into materials that are water and heat resistant, perhaps antibacterial, and even machine washable. Whether it's vinyl, leather, wood, or foil, it would be wise to make sure that your materials can endure a significant amount of distress to get the most quality use out of them. Don't worry, we'll get into the nitty-gritty intricacies of material choice further into this book.

You now know just how useful a Cricut can be. In this chapter, you learned that you can use a die-cutter for arts and crafts, to make useful tools, to create decorations and accessories for your home, to make jewelry, and to create gifts for yourself and your family—you can even create entire pieces of clothing! A Cricut also gives you the possibility to make your own office supplies and promotional brand products— that is, if you choose the right one.

Since you know how a Cricut machine works, as well as what you can and can't use it for, it's time to choose the one that works best for you. The next chapter will review the most popular Cricut die-cutter models so that you can choose the one that has the exact features and functions you need.

Chapter 2:

Choose the Right Cricut: Types and Features of the Most Popular Cricut Models

Now that you know what you can expect from a Cricut machine (and you've hopefully decided to obtain one), let's review the most popular models so that you can choose the best one for your intended purposes. In this chapter, you'll learn all about the different features and performance of the three distinct Cricut models that everyone is raving about. Buying your first Cricut shouldn't be done in a rush. Before deciding to commit to your first die-cutter machine, you'll have to look into your unique needs.

The first thing you should know is that, although the machines have different features, they can be easily operated from the same software. Depending on your skill level in graphic design, computer skills, and budgeting, you can work with more beginner-friendly designs and functions, and as your skills and abilities advance, you can proceed to purchase designs and use graphic design skills to tweak and adjust them. The entry-level designs and projects are best done with ready-to-use projects that you get when you purchase the machine and when you buy subscriptions from different software.

Image importing is done easily, and you can create your own designs in Photoshop or Adobe Illustrator, convert them into one of the required formats, and then load them to the software. Whichever software you choose will give you a certain level of possibility to adjust and clean up designs so that any imperfections are removed. Once you're done with designing, you can then send the image to the machine, and it will proceed to do as it's told. However, you will need to place your cutting material onto a sticky mat first so that it can pass through the cutter and lie fixed and stable during cutting. Your machine will come with a basic mat, but if you need a specialized mat, like for cutting balsa wood, you'll have to get it separately.

If you're worried about the proper material to use with your Cricut, relax; the brand offers a wide range of materials for you to use, from card and paper to vinyl, chipboard, iron-on, and fabric. In fact, if you're a beginner, using the brand's consumables is most likely to produce quality results. It's also important to know that you can use consumable scraps. You don't have to pull out a new sheet each time you're printing, which reduces waste and guarantees you get the most use out of your materials.

Now that you know this bit of crucial information, let's compare several Cricut models and review their features.

The Cricut Explore Air 2

The Cricut Explore Air 2 is the brand's oldest die-cutter. Despite the age of the model, it remains the top runner when it comes to cutting with accuracy and versatility. Both in terms of price and functionality, the Explore Air 2 gives you a happy middle between the Joy's simplicity and the Maker's robustness. The Explore Air 2 is a great option for beginners and intermediate artists alike, as it doesn't require the advanced skills that you'll need to work with the Maker. The Explore Air 2 was the brand's first machine to have the ability to connect via Bluetooth, but this feature has since been added to the other two models as well (Peterson, C., 2019).

An upside to the Explore Air 2 is that it can cut a majority of lighter materials. You can use it on iron-on, cards, vinyl, paper, and light-to-medium fabrics. However, if you wish to cut fabrics, you're going to have to use fusible interfacing to stabilize the material first. Given the extent of the machine's abilities, the Explore Air 2 is a great option for hobby crafters who don't want to spend extra money on the Maker. It is also a great option if you plan on cutting a lot of vinyl, card, or paper, but you aren't too interested in fabrics or wood. However, it does have some limitations compared to the Maker.

While the Explore Air 2 features an admirable level of accuracy and cutting, it doesn't have the Maker's breadth or versatility when it comes to features. It includes four different add-ons for writing and can cut over 100 different materials, but is still quite limited compared to the Maker, which is the brand's flagship product.

To sum up, Explore Air 2 can provide a decent level of cutting and writing, and it is best suited for intermediate hobby crafters. If you want to occasionally make your own decorations, invitations, cards, or otherwise just have fun with cutting, the Explore Air 2 is your best bet. However, if you want a machine that can give you a more refined level of craftsmanship, you're going to have to invest in one of the more powerful Cricut models.

The Cricut Maker

The Cricut Maker is the finest available smart die-cutter. It's the brand's staple product, featuring the widest range of possibilities, add-ons, and works with tougher materials compared to the Joy and Explore Air 2. The machine can apply much greater pressure compared to others, which increases the scope of materials that you can use with it. It features the brand's adaptive tool system, which lets you fit more add-ons, blades, and tools than other models.

This model features a rotary blade that lets you cut non-bonded fabric, a knife blade, that you can use to cut through balsa wood and leather, a scoring and double scoring wheels for scoring card paper. The machine also comes with a debossing tip, which lets you add debossing on your paper and carts, an engraving tip, which works on leather, Perspex, and metal.

This machine also lets you create decorative wavy edges by using a wavy blade, and it also comes with a perforation blade so that you can cut perforated edges. Your projects can further be enhanced with foil accents, which you can make using the machine's foil transfer tool.

Aside from offering the biggest number of features and add-ons, this model is also safe to purchase for future upgrades. Whenever the brand designs new tools, they will be created in a way to fit the Maker. Although you'll have to make a significant investment to buy this machine, you can rest assured that it will never become outdated.

The Maker works with the biggest number of materials out of the bunch. You can use it with the finest fabrics like organza and silk, and it can also work with crepe and tissue paper. Along with that, you can rely on it to cut through harder materials like balsa wood, chipboard, leather, and even heavy denim. However, you still have to comply with certain sheet size and thickness restrictions. Like the Explore Air 2, this model also cuts up to 11 inches in width, and it can only cut materials that are up to 2.4mm thick.

The Maker has one important upside compared to the others, and that is that it can cut un-bonded fabric thanks to its rotary blade tool. To sum up, the Maker is the best option for those who are serious about their craftsmanship, those who are using their machine for business purposes, and those hoping to run their own business with items they create using the Maker.

The Cricut Joy

The Cricut Joy is the brand's newest machine. It came out in February 2020 and features a compact size. It measures 8 inches in width and weighs only 3.85 pounds. It is highly convenient for working at home, as its compact size allows you to plug it in and operate on your small kitchen or home office table, and you can also tuck it away safely when you're not using it; you can place it in a cupboard or on a shelf, and pull it out and plug it in just as easily when you want to use it again.

The machine doesn't feature any buttons, meaning that you can fully operate it from your computer. This makes it even more convenient to use if you have kids and you don't want to risk them touching or otherwise intervening with your work. Plus, the Joy has the same level of accuracy as other Cricut models, which makes it a complete wing for anyone working in a small space or in need of a portable cutter.

Despite its convenient size, the Joy can handle similarly demanding tasks to other Cricut models, and even more. In fact, the machine's size doesn't intervene with its length. It can cut much longer designs, ranging from 4-foot continuous to 20-foot repeated designs. This makes it great for wall decals, party decorations, and simple banners. However, its cutting width is much more modest compared to the other models. The Joy can cut a maximum of 4.25 inches in width, while others can cut up to 11.5 inches.

You can use the Joy to cut the majority of common crafting materials. It will work well with sticker paper, vinyl, cards, paper, and iron-on. Although there are some limitations that stem from the size of the machine, it is currently the brand's only model that can cut without needing a mat. It has two special features, Smart Iron-On and Smart Vinyl, which make it easier for you to use the machine.

Another specialty option called the "Card Mat" lets you put folded cards into the mat before cutting. With this option, you get the save some time cutting your cards, plus achieve more precise alignment. The first major downside to the Joy, however, is that it can't cut through balsa wood, chipboard, fabric, or other heavy materials. The second downside is that it doesn't print or cut.

Unlike other models, the Joy is best suited for everyday use at home and for your family. It can be very helpful in making custom storage labels, birthday cards, and other simple projects using light materials. It is also the most beginner-friendly Cricut, as it is most convenient for those who are just learning to work with die-cutters and their software. In conclusion, the Cricut Joy is most ideal for beginners, those in need of craftwork on-the-go, and those who are just starting out.

Chapter 3:

Cricut Complex Operations

After the initial excitement you feel regarding the possibilities of this apparatus, you may experience some fear and concern about how to actually perform the complex operations involved. With that in mind, this chapter includes a short guide for performing complex operations on your die-cutter. After you finish this chapter, you should be able to master your machine and make your visions come to life.

Cricut Explore Air 2

Let's begin with the Cricut Explore Air 2. This machine is capable of two very popular functions, which are the "write then cut" and "draw then cut". These two options let you personalize and embellish your projects using pens and markers. Your machine comes with multiple markers and pens for writing and drawing your designs, and you can also get additional ones on the brand's website.

Print Then Cut

This function allows you to write on the material before cutting out a shape. It's great for adding quotes, phrases, lyrics, and pretty much anything that comes to mind to your cardstock designs. To start writing then cutting, you first need to choose a basic shape for cutting. After selecting an image to cut, insert it into your project and Design Space. Remember to frequently click the save button so that you don't lose your work (Peterson, 2019).

After writing your text, position it to where you want it to be on the design and also rotate if needed to further adjust the look. Click "Text" and select a font for your written content. Choose "Filter" and then "Writing" to browse through writing styles and fonts. Select your font, and type your text into the text box. Then, select the text box, and choose the preferred alignment option. To show Design Space where to start writing the text, select your text and tag, and then click "Attach".

To start the process of printing then cutting, finally click "Make it", and your machine will start doing its work. You can adjust the number of copies that are to be created by clicking the up or down arrow, and then clicking "Apply" once you've made your choice.

When you're ready to start printing, you need to choose the right material setting, and then load the correct pen and the appropriate blade. Press "Go", and the machine will start creating your design.

Draw Then Cut

Drawing and cutting images on the Explore Air 2 follows the same series of steps as writing than cutting. If you don't want to make your own images, you can browse the software and find a photo from the brand's own collection. Better yet, the Explore Air 2 comes with multiple images that are pre-designed and great for attaching, drawing, and cutting. Of course, drawing then cutting removes the part of the process that requires you to write text, choose fonts, and make other related decisions (Peterson, 2019).

If you're a beginner, perhaps the best way to go about drawing then cutting would be to find the available images in Design Space. Use the search box to browse appropriate images by typing in keywords and search terms that are related to your project. You'll easily find these by clicking "Images" and searching through them. Make sure to select "Art type" and "Draw only" before saving the project.

Great job! You now know how to print, draw, and cut with your Cricut Explore Air 2. As you can see, the process isn't all that difficult. A couple of things to keep in mind are the following tips:

- Make sure that your chosen design works well with the material.
- Don't forget to adjust the material settings before cutting so that the machine uses the correct amount of speed and pressure.
- Think about how the material color and texture will work with your pen and marker colors.

Cricut Maker

Now that you know how to work with the Explore Air 2, let's start looking into the more versatile functions and options that are included with the Maker. You can convert any given design into a writing, drawing, or cutting project. You can start learning by trying out new designs and playing with functions to see what kind of a result you'll get. Your Cricut will come with a set of pens that cover all the basic colors and styles. If you wish to expand your choice, you can order more pens and sets from the brand's website.

Your Maker will come with multiple standard-tip pens in a variety of colors. These pens have fine points that work great for making and drawing designs, as they're small enough to create distinct intricate details and crisp lines. Glitter pens, on the other hand, have ballpoints that glide over the paper and create consistent lines and fine accents. Moreover, you can use calligraphy pens with your machine, which come in two different nib sizes. Aside from this, you can draw with metallic pens that have slightly bigger nibs, creating an effect that is more similar to a marker. They are medium-sized.

Aside from these pens, the Maker also carries infusible ink markers and pens. These pens have a heat-set that binds the ink with the material and creates a more durable design. Remember to use only the brand's pens and markers; off-brand tools require special adapters that are known to work, but the quality of the result cannot be guaranteed. For example, you can expect the ink to not flow as smoothly with off-brands, and they could bleed or result in an inconsistent line.

When working in Design Space, all you need to do is mark a line for drawing, and the software will command the machine to start creating your image. But, how to create a drawing before applying it to the material? Here's what you need to do. After importing the image into your Design Space, select a layer of the image that you wish to draw. When you click the layer icon, you can choose between a printer, scissors, or a pen. In this case, you should choose the pen icon, which will open a palette for you to choose the color that will be drawn on.

You can repeat this process for each individual layer. Selecting "Draw" or a layer will show a choice of colors on the screen, and you can now choose whether to use the same color for all layers or opt for multiple colors on different layers. The software will offer the colors you've used previously, and you can also access a larger color palette to make a choice.

Setting up your Maker for drawing requires the same steps mentioned in the previous section. Once you start creating your design, you'll receive a message to change pen colors when needed. This way, you can create drawing designs out of pretty much any line, shape, or image. However, not all draw lines can be used as cut shapes. This is important to remember when planning the cut shape for your design. Depending on the shape, some lines might result in the scrapped paper.

If you want to locate designs you worked on previously, you can open "Images" on your Canvas, and then type in a search term or a keyword. This will show you the pictures that match the keywords that you've created previously. You can also choose "Cartridges" to browse through available design sets, which have all been specifically created for drawing.

In order to do complex drawings with your Cricut Maker, go through the following steps. Attach the drawing lines to keep a whole layout. Make sure to use the "Attach" function, because grouping lines only serves to move the pieces on the Canvas together.

Next, designate the position of the drawing line. Here, you have two choices; you can attach your drawing to the Canvas layout, which will give you a background paper surrounding to overview your drawings, or you can work on a specific cut design. You can refer to this design for drawing, as long as you're making sure that your drawing is attached to your cut design.

The next step is to move the design on the Canvas before you start cutting it. If you haven't chosen a specific cut shape to attach your drawing, you can move it around the final mat view. This will help you position your drawing on the mat where you need it, or to preserve the cutting sheet in case you plan to use it multiple times. Be careful to place the drawing exactly where you need to before drawing. Next, check out how the lines look on your screen. They will appear on the screen the same way as they will on paper. This also means that if there are any areas where the drawing is overlapping, it will overlap on the paper as well. This is especially important since there's currently no way for you to cut out parts of lines.

If this is your first time drawing, or if you're using a new set of pens, make sure to test out the pens before you start making your project. This will help you see how colors look on the paper or multiple types of paper and paper colors, how their color translates onto the paper and whether it's bold enough, etc. This is particularly important for glitter and metallic pens, where seeing how saturated they come out helps you plan your drawing.

Cricut Joy

Now let us delve into all of the beauty that you can create with your Cricut Joy. This machine can cut infusible ink materials, paper, vinyl, and many more materials, which opens you up to an endless amount of options to design and cut projects. Despite being smaller and slightly limiting in terms of materials and functions, your Cricut Joy can still write, draw, and cut. It can work with pre-made designs, as well as the ones you make on your own in Design Space. Joy's small size makes it easy to work on various projects without taking up the extra space you would need with your Explore or Maker.

If you only wish to be creative around the house or print and cut smaller projects like stickers and labels, then the Cricut Joy is everything you'll need. When it comes to printing, drawing, and cutting, the Joy requires the same set of steps you'd use with the other two models. Still, it's worthwhile to try and explain one simple project that you can do with your Cricut Joy. So, we will now go over how to create work with a label using your Cricut Joy.

Cutting labels with your machine will require five minutes in total. You'll need a sheet of Cricut Joy Smart Vinyl, some transfer tape, and a weeding tool. Of course, you'll also need a finished design for your label that's ready to cut and print. With the following instructions, you should be able to get this accomplished.

First, open the text tool in a Design Space blank document. You'll find it in the left sidebar. This will pull up a text entry box. Once your text box is opened, insert the desired text and choose the preferred font. If you're printing labels, it would be wise to choose a clean, read-friendly font. Next, adjust the size of the font by dragging the text box's corners. This way, you can resize the label to the exact dimensions you need. Once you're done designing, click "Make it".

Load the vinyl into the machine without the mat this time. The screen will guide you through further steps. The Cricut will then recognize the material and set it in place. Now that the material is loaded, the software will start after you hit the "Go" button, which is located at the bottom of your screen. Then, your machine will start cutting.

Once the cutting is finished, the material will be unloaded on its own. Remove the cut from the mat, which is best done by pulling the material back. Use a weeding tool to remove excess pieces of vinyl from letters. Set your cut-out word onto a piece of transfer tape, which will secure the label and make it easier to set onto a container.

After sticking the label with a transfer tape, peel it off and throw it away, which will leave a clear, sticky layer to transfer onto the label. Once the letters adhere to the tape, you're done! All that's left to do is pull the tape back, which will pull up the letters, and then press them onto the container.

Finally, tape the letters onto the container, rub over them with your finger, and pull the tape back to leave only the letters on the container surface.

Great work! You now know how to draw, print, and cut with your Cricut machine(s). As you can see, the steps are quite similar regardless of the machine you choose.

Throughout this chapter, you have learned how to perform basic and more complex operations on different Cricut models. However, the most complex part of the process is for you to create your unique designs and import your own projects and images. In the next chapter, you'll learn how to do just that. We'll review Design Space, and break down its basic functions.

Chapter 4:

Maintenance of the Cricut

Machine

Cricut machines require regular maintenance. Although they're high quality, regular use and time spent sitting on different surfaces will lead to dust and material particles collecting. You may also notice that grease from the machine will begin to build on the carriage track. To prolong your machine's lifespan, it's recommended that you clean it regularly. This process is quite easy, not requiring a lot of effort.

Before cleaning your machine, make sure that it's disconnected from power. You can clean it easily using a soft cloth. All you need to do is dampen it with a glass cleaner and go over the machine, making sure that you've removed all of the dust. Likewise, you can clean up any paper particles that have built up due to static electricity. If you notice a slight grease build-up over the carriage bar, then you can remove it with a cotton swab or a damp cloth. Make sure to apply only gentle surface cleaners; avoid using acetone, bleach, and other harsh chemicals that might damage the machine's plastic surfaces.

How to apply grease to your Cricut machine: Before applying the grease onto your Cricut machine, you first need to turn it off. Then, you need to push the Cut Smart carriage slowly to the left and clean it with a tissue. Wipe the previous grease residue around the bar, and then push the carriage to the right. Repeat the process of moving the bar and cleaning until you've removed all of the old grease residues.

Then, move the carriage to the machine's center, and open the lubrication package. Squeeze out a small drop of grease onto a cotton swab, and apply a coating of it onto a quarter of a ring surrounding the bar on both sides of the carriage. Move the carriage from left to right to distribute the grease across the bar evenly. Since the machine has a unique design, it's best to use their brand lubrication packages. If you wish to get one on your own, I recommend calling their customer service and checking what type and substitute brands work the best with your particular machine.

Although the machine and its add-ons aren't high maintenance or particularly dangerous, you should make sure to keep your grease package away from children. If any accidents occurred, the grease may cause irritation on the skin and the eyes. In that case, rinse it right away and make sure to wash your hands after handling it.

Now, let's look at some model-specific Cricut maintenance must-know.

Cricut Explore Air 1

Now that you've used your machine for a while, you may notice some debris starting to gather. Although the Explore Air 2 doesn't get exposed to as many materials as the Maker, all of the paper, vinyl, glitter, and cardstock may leave your machine looking dirty, and no one likes working with a dirty machine, right? The previous section gave you a couple of general Cricut cleaning and maintenance tips. Now, you'll now learn a couple of things that you should and shouldn't do when cleaning your cutter (Sund, 2010; Peterson, 2019.):

Don't use alcohol-based cleaners. They might damage the plastic surfaces of the Cricut Explore or corrode its metal parts. Always use the most gentle cleaner you can find. Also, make sure not to spray the cleaner directly onto the surface of the machine, because it could cause drops of liquid to build up inside of it and cause trouble later on.

Remove residue from the blade housing. You can move the housing from one side to another to pick up the debris. However, don't over-clean or wipe off the grease that's on the bar that holds the housing. This grease is a lubricant, and you shouldn't remove it completely as it would rid the machine of its lubrication. Also, make sure not to touch the gear chain at the back of the machine.

Never ignore grinding. If used and cleaned properly, your machine shouldn't make any funny noises. If you hear grinding coming from the unit, consult the brand's customer support for proper evaluation and lubrication instructions.

Never leave the surface wet. Once you're done cleaning the exterior panels of your Explore Air 2, make sure to completely dry the surfaces with a clean cloth. If you leave it damp, it could further attract dust from the air and leave stains as the surface dries. It is also a safety hazard since electricity should never run through a damp machine.

Don't use brushes, sponges, or other cleaning tools. You might feel tempted to give your machine an extra scrubbing if it gets really dirty, but resist the urge to do it. Instead, persist in lightly cleaning with a damp cloth. If your Cricut is extremely dirty, switch between multiple soft cloths instead of doing any harsh cleaning. On top of that, never use scratchy cleaners; they could damage or corrode the plastic and metal surfaces of your machine.

Be professional around your machine. Your Cricut doesn't care for your vocabulary, but it won't put up with any foods or drinks in its close proximity. It might sound exaggerated, but refraining from eating and drinking around your machine will prevent crumbs from getting anywhere near its sensitive parts and, of course, it will eliminate the possibility of ruining your machine due to spilling.

Keep your machine in the shade. Although Cricuts aren't seriously sensitive to light, keeping them in direct sunlight for an extended period of time might contribute to overheating, damage to the plastic parts of the machine, and it could even cause some of its components to deform.

Care for your cutting mat. Your Cricut will deal with multitudes of fabrics, and hopefully, give you plenty of repeated uses on a single mat. If maintained properly, a single mat could endure anywhere from 25 to 40 full cuts. Make sure to replace the mat as soon as you notice that the materials aren't sticking to it. If you notice that it is starting to get dirty, you can give it a gentle cleaning with a wet wipe. However, avoid cleaning too much so that you don't remove the adhesive.

Cricut Maker

As the brand's most complex machine, the Cricut Maker is likely to handle the most stress. For this reason, I am going to give you slightly more input on how to care for the particular parts and features of the machine. The said instructions, of course, can apply to other models as well, but it's most likely that you won't have to follow through with all of the instructions for them. Instead, do so only as needed.

Given that the Maker will be your biggest die-cutter investment, adhering to these maintenance principles will significantly affect the quality of its performance. As you'll learn not only in this book but also when using the Maker, neglecting to clean it might affect its cutting accuracy and even cause chipping of the materials as they're being cut. You want to avoid this at all costs. A couple of important maintenance tips, which we will now go over, will grant laser-precision in cutting, printing, and drawing.

Notice the warning signs. There are a couple of indications that your Maker needs a thorough cleaning, and you should take them seriously as soon as they appear. First, you may notice that your cuts are getting bunched up in certain places or that they appear to be torn or ragged. This doesn't always mean that your machine has started to break down or that it needs repair or replacement, but it does mean that you should take immediate action, even if deviations in cutting are as small as minor inaccuracies.

Give your machine a break. As most people consider the Maker to be the most robust of all die-cutters, they're more likely to expose it to long and hard work. If you've been pushing your machine to its maximum, and it's now starting to show signs of distress, the first thing you need to do is lower the stress. Slow down the working speed, alleviate the pressure, and cut back on the blade depth. If these steps don't yield any improvement in the machine's performance, you should replace the blade and the mat. After you've taken these steps, you should see a visible improvement.

Give your machine space. If there's apparent underperformance despite taking the previous steps, make sure that your machine is properly placed. It should stand on a flat, firm surface with plenty of breathing space around it. It's possible that, over time, you've gotten used to storing extra tools and supplies around your machine and that some of the material scraps or tools have gotten under the machine, causing it to overheat. Lift it up, make sure that the space underneath and around it is clean and clear, and be certain it continues to be like that.

Check cables and cords. Despite your best efforts, it's still possible for some cords and cables to tangle or tear. Unplug all of the cables from the machine and device, check their condition, and replace those that appear damaged. Once you're certain that all of them are in good shape, plug everything back in. This will ensure that the device, machine, and Bluetooth adapters have a proper connection.

Check your blade. After making sure that the blade holder is properly cleaned, entertain the possibility that the blade might be damaged. Check it out underneath the magnifying glass to see if it became blunt or chipped. Replace, sharpen, or clean the blade if needed.

Clean the working space. Cleaning the machine alone won't improve its performance much if its environment is damp or dusty. If your workspace contains shelves and stacks of materials, give all of them a good dusting to prevent any debris from getting into the machine.

Check the cutting strip. By now, you've probably understood how important it is to clean the blade, bar, and rollers. However, don't forget to check the Maker's cutting strip every once in a while. A cutting strip is also a place where adhesive, dust, and debris can pile up.

Heavy-duty grip rollers. Grip rollers are set right below the cutter's front. They are a rough surface, which pulls the mat inside and out of the cutter. It's very important for these rollers to be clean and debris-free, or else they could be directly responsible for material tearing and sloppy cuts. The matter is made worse by the fact that grip rollers are difficult to clean. If you're stuck with dirty rollers, your only choice is to grab a magnifying glass and tweezers and carefully pick out specks of debris. After you're finished with this step, give them another thorough clean with a Q-tip or a cotton swab.

Careful handling. Prevention is the best way to ensure that your machine consistently performs well. You'll protect its grit rollers by making sure to resurface the mats carefully so that no adhesive touches other surfaces of the machine. While it's safe to use tape on the surfaces of the mat, keep it away from its edges so that it doesn't get stuck inside the rollers.

Cricut Joy

As the brand's simplest machine, the Cricut Joy should serve you well for a very long time if used as intended. The same maintenance rules and tips apply to this model as the two previous ones. To preserve the machine and extend its lifespan, you should follow a couple of additional tips.

Use only Cricut's materials. The Joy isn't intended for robust use and production, so why risk using papers, mats, and add-ons that aren't best suited to the brand? Stick to sheets, mats, and other tools and supplies found on the brand's website, and you can expect your machine to last long while performing well.

Contact customer support when unsure about the right settings.
As you have learned by now, Cricut settings don't follow a predictable logic in terms of a series of steps and terminology. You're given a lot of choices, from blade pressure to speed. If you're ever unsure about which ones to use, don't hesitate to call customer support and ask. Better safe than sorry, after all.

Choose lighter projects. Sometimes, the failure to cut out clean, intricate patterns isn't on the machine; it can also happen if you're printing small but very detailed patterns. If you're cutting these patterns on harder materials like cardstock, and they don't seem to come out well, try choosing a different material instead of forcing the machine to perform an operation that's clearly putting too much pressure on it.

In this chapter, you have learned how to take good care of your Cricut machine(s). Whichever model you choose, remember to treat it with care and as intended. You received thorough instructions for how to clean your die-cutter and prevent any damage. If you clean your machine and workspace regularly and adhere to the user guide, you will create countless clean, precise, and beautiful projects.

Now that you know how to care for your cutter, let's learn how to create designs. The next chapter will show you how to work in Design Space.

Chapter 5:

Cricut and Design Space

While you're thinking about which Cricut machine to get, let's start learning how to set it up and work in Design Space. While there are multiple software programs that are compatible with Cricut die-cutters, the main advantage of using this one is that it's free. Also, this software is recommended by the brand and features pre-made designs, templates, and projects that you'll find to be invaluable as a beginner.

In this chapter, you'll learn the basics of working in Design Space, as well as how to set up and connect your Cricut for easy, seamless operating.

Basic Design Space Terms

Before you start learning about more complex Cricut operations, let's introduce you to the basic terms you'll need to know first (Yuikrd, 2020):

- Alignment is a function that will set multiple items on your Canvas either in the center, top or bottom, or left- or right-hand corner.
- Attachment is a tool that allows you to set two images, as well as attach score lines and lettering to the images that you're cutting.
- The arrangement is a function that allows you to move images in between, behind, or in front of other images.

- Canvas is a visual workspace that provides you with the ability to arrange and design vectors and prints.
- Color syncing lets you consolidate colors used on one project to get a cohesive result for multiple projects.
- Contouring lets you edit portions of image layers so that they're not cut out.
- The Go Button/Cricut Cut is a logo button on the cutter's left side. Pressing this button will initiate cutting.
- Cut lines mark the shape outlines of each layer that is to be cut.
- The Cut Screen is a screen that presents itself when the machine is cutting.
- A cutting mat is a surface that you stick your material onto to load it into the machine. When using a Cricut, you'll choose a green cutting mat for vinyl, a purple one for wood, a pink one for fabric, and a blue one for paper.

Now, let's examine some of the Cricut functions that are necessary to operate the machine.

How to Set the Blade

Make sure that the housing of your blade sits on the B clamp's top surface to properly contact the material. Operating the machine won't be possible if the blade doesn't properly contact the material, which can happen if it's seated too high. Next, when closing the clamp, make sure to shut the left one first and the right clamp second. If you follow this guideline, the clamps will be set snug around the blade. The plastic tab is best closed by holding the left arm in place and then swinging your right arm around. Apply gentle pressure to close the tab. You'll know that you've set the blade correctly if both clamps align.

Know Your Material Limits

Your cutter will perform best if you abide by some material thickness guidelines. You can use the thickest materials with the Cricut Maker, which can cut 2.4mm or 3.32-inch thick materials. This goes for both its knife and rotary blades.

You'll have to be connected to the internet to operate the designing software that comes with the machine. The software itself is interned-based, but some of the apps, like those for IOS devices, also operate with offline features.

Set up Your Cricut Die-Cutter

Before you head out to do anything with these die-cutters, let's examine general instructions for how to set them up. This process is the same for all of the most popular models across the board, but it differs slightly across different devices.

Cricut Windows/Mac Set-Up

Setting up the Cricut on your laptop or desktop begins with plugging in your machine and turning it on. Next, you'll use a Bluetooth or a USB cord to connect the machine with your computer. After that, visit the brand's website setup page and simply follow the manufacturer's instructions. After this, all you need to do is download and install the designing software. Once the installation is complete, the software will invite you to start making your first project.

Cricut Android and IOS Set-Up

After plugging in and turning on your machine, pair it with the device via Bluetooth. After that, you need to download the Design Space app and follow the instructions for installation. Open the app, set up your account, and head to Machine Setup>New Machine Setup. Follow the instructions until the installed software invites you to start making your project.

Your machines will come with built-in Bluetooth modules and some that don't come with a Bluetooth adapter, so pairing them shouldn't be a problem. To pair the machine with a Windows computer, you'll need to make sure that the machine is within 10-15 feet of the device. Check your device manager to make sure that the Bluetooth is enabled, or get a specialty device that enables your device to connect with others. Add the machine's Bluetooth device in the Devices and Printer from the Control panel, and let your device detect the machine's Bluetooth.

Once the device is detected, select the machine's name and double-click to finalize the pairing. You should follow similar steps for a Mac device. After you make sure that the adapter has been inserted, open System Preferences and look for the Bluetooth option. Turn on the Bluetooth if it has been turned off. Select the device and click Pair. If you're asked to enter a code, type in 0000 and click Pair.

On Android and IOS devices, you first need to make sure that the machine is in close proximity to the other Bluetooth. Make sure that the machine is turned on with an inserted Bluetooth adapter. Open your Settings app, and turn on Bluetooth communication. Find your machine's name on the list and tap it to pair devices. If required, type in the 0000 code as the PIN, and finish by tapping Done.

To pair your Android device, first make sure that both devices are within range and that the wireless adapter is inserted. To do this, start by opening the Settings app. You will find this app on your screen. Tap the Bluetooth icon and turn it on. Find the machine's Bluetooth name on the screen, and select it to start pairing. Use the same four-digit password as mentioned earlier if required.

You may be wondering what the designing software's features are and how you operate them. A function known as Slice Weld will remove any overlapping cut lines and join multiple material layers. It will also cut a shape from another and delete parts of an image that you don't wish to be cut. You will use the functions Attach and Detach to separate objects into individual layers, and from here, you can proceed with scoring, drawing, and cutting lines independently.

The Detach function removes projects overall. The Attach function also fixes objects to the Canvas so that they appear in the same layout as on your screen. This function will assure that different layered objects stay together as you move them onto the Canvas, as well as once you transfer them to your Prepare screen.

To further control layered cutting, a function called Flatten will separate different layers when you're using Print then Cut and create multiple individual layers. In contrast, the function called Unflatten will combine multiple layers into one during the said operation. It also allows you to hide or show individual contours, lines, or cut lines.

The Contour function hides or reveals individual layers. It allows you to choose the parts of specific layers to score, write, cut, or print, as well as select those parts of a layer you wish to omit from this process. When working with multilayered images, a function called Visible/Hidden lets you ungroup the image first, and then group objects together so that you can resize all of them on your Canvas.

Grouping separate layers will let you move and adjust their size independently, while ungrouping allows you to move individual positions of letters. This function, however, won't attach objects to one another, but rather only let you make duplicates of a selected image.

Operating Your Design Canvas

The Canvas is a virtual space on your screen that is utilized for adding, editing, and designing projects, text, and images. When starting to work on a project from scratch, you need to open your Design Panel and click the New icon to start a new project. To visualize a finished project, use the tab Templates. The Projects tab lets you browse, choose, and cut different projects, which includes both those that came with the machine and the ones you made on your own.

The Images tab allows you to perform the same operations on images, whether you've uploaded them on your own or they came with the installation. The Text tab lets you add words and phrases to your projects, and visiting the Shapes tab will reveal basic score lines, triangles, squares, and circles that can be added to your Canvas. The Upload tab lets you add a variety of different image files to the Canvas.

How to Navigate Design Space

The Menu lets you browse the software entirely and switch pathways from Canvas to Home. It also leads you to features like Settings, Cartridges, Machine Setup, and others. When you start a new project, its name will appear in the Project Name tab, which will also be named Untitled if you haven't yet given it a title.

Once you're finished working on your project, you can click on Save, which will make your project available across multiple devices, or you can choose Save As if you want to rename your project. Once you're finished with designing your project and you're ready to put it in motion, you need to click Make It and then prepare mats as your project will be sent to the machine.

Unless your projects have already been cut, you can use the Edit bar to make some final adjustments. The main functions include Undo and Redo, which either erase or recover some of the previous actions.

When working on your Canvas, the function known as Linetype allows you to set up the interaction between the material and the mat. Here, you can prepare the machine for scoring, drawing, and cutting. Choosing Cut will start the cutting process, while Draw will enable the machine to draw the object presented on the Canvas with a pen. If you choose Score, a scoring tool will be used for your design. However, if you want to add variety to your design (e.g., if you want some of your lines cut and others to be drawn on with a couple of them scored), you can use the function Linetype swatch. This will allow you to add different attributes to project layers.

Aside from the basic operations, you can match the project with material colors using the "Materials Colors" pallet. The Basic colors will open a palette of basic colors, and the Advanced will open a custom color picker from which you can either enter a color code or pick the shade you wish to use manually.

Choosing Draw Attributes is possible when you select the Draw Linetype, and this option lets you choose a pen type and available colors from the drop-down menu. The Fill option gives you the ability to choose a pattern or a color to fill your image layers when you're doing Print Then Cut. When the option No Fill is on, it means that you haven't chosen any colors to fill your images. If this is the case, the layer will only be cut. Choosing the Print option will open color and pattern choices and display fill swatches for your print layers. If you wish to restore an original Print layer, you should click Original Artwork.

Choosing a Pattern option will let you apply a pattern to your text layer or image. You can narrow your pattern search by filtering by color. After you've chosen the desired pattern, you can then use Edit Pattern tools to edit the pattern orientation and scale. This feature also has an Edit function, which allows you to copy, paste, and cut images from the clipboard.

Choosing the Slice option will divide two overlapping layers into individual parts, while the Weld option removes overlapping lines and joins separate layers together to form one object. The option Sync Panel consolidates colors and reduces the number of materials that are needed. You can sync an image by dragging and dropping it onto another layer. The option Zoom lets you get a closer look at an object or zoom out from it for a better overview.

Because the software is cloud-based, you can connect it to multiple computers and IOS devices. Any changes you make on a single device will update on other devices as well. The software also lets you disable gridlines and toggle them as needed. You can set this up by accessing your Account menu>Settings>Canvas Grid to adjust your preferences. The Settings menu also contains Keyboard shortcuts which tell you about specific keys to press on your keyboard for particular operations. The design software also lets you change measurement units to metric, which is a setting you can access in your Account menu.

The software distinguishes two types of images that you can upload, which are Vector and Basic. The Basic images include common image file types. You can upload these files as a single layer, and you'll have a broad option to further edit these images along the way.

Great job! You now know the basics of working in Design Space, which will make your beginner projects a lot easier to create! As you have probably noticed, Design Space isn't all that difficult to use. You mainly will utilize it to upload already-made images, and if you feared that you will have to design prints from scratch, you now know that you don't have to. The software's library gives you plenty of free designs to use, and even established Cricut crafters and business owners would rather choose pre-made designs than purchasing new ones.

The beauty and the main purpose of Design Space is that it gives you an overview of how your image is positioned on the mat, and it also provides you with plenty of options to adjust and personalize your work. As you've learned, it's extremely important to choose proper settings when working in Design Space. Material and operation settings, font and image sizes, alignment, mirroring, layers, and grouping and ungrouping images all affect the quality of your product.

This chapter might feel overwhelming if you've just heard about Design Space, but as soon as you test the software, you'll realize there's a method to its madness. All the functions and items to check out will fall into place, as you'll learn about their real impact and value. So, don't feel intimidated by Design Space! Give it a chance, and I promise that you'll love it after your first project.

Chapter 6:

Materials That Can Be Worked On

Cricut Explore Air 2

The Cricut Explore Air 2 isn't the brand's most popular machine, but it is one of the favorites for those intermediate crafters who need a more serious tool; however, it's not as powerful as the Maker. Although it can't cut as many materials as the Maker, it still gives you enough versatility for pretty much any project you set your mind to doing.

Its limitations in working with sturdier and extremely softer materials don't mean that you need to completely give up on projects that need said materials. You can look for alternatives that serve the same purpose, or cut the said materials by hand as an alternative.

That being said, the Cricut Explore Air 2 is mainly popular with paper crafters who like creating stickers, posters, postcards, or adhesive iron-ons to decorate sturdy materials and fabrics. If you belong to this group and you don't need to do extra work to complete the project, the Explore Air 2 will be the right machine for you.

Regardless of its limitations in the choice of materials, you still have over a hundred options to choose from. You will be able to make banners, pictures, lamps, decorated pillowcases and linens, pendants, and so much more.

Chipboard is the sturdiest material that the Explore Air 2 can cut, and you can use it for a multitude of advanced projects. The other popular materials that you can cut with this machine include cardstock, vinyl, paper, glitter materials, iron-on, and others. The list goes on to include various types of vinyl, from holographic to chalkboard and glitter, foil and glitter iron-on, and adhesive foil.

This range of materials allows you to create decorations, cards, and various accessories for Valentine's Day, Christmas, birthdays, weddings, and other events. Although it won't be able to cut fabric, which would be a significant saver of time and money, you will be able to create adhesive and iron-on images, quotes, and patterns to add creativity and uniqueness to your craft.

Another important thing about the Explore Air 2 is that it can cut through leather, which increases your range of possibilities. This machine enables you to create leather jewelry and other accessories, as well as luxury office supplies like planners, and even quality bags and wallets. If you combine the machine's ability to emboss and score with some detailed eye for paper design, you can even make fine journals from scratch.

Wood pallet signs are another great piece of artwork that you can make with this machine. Of course, you will need additional tools, like a hot press. For these types of projects, you'll have to provide your own wooden supplies, and you can apply all sorts of quotes, letters, and images onto the wood for quality, aesthetically-pleasing results.

You've probably heard of crazy successful planner supply Etsy shops, and they are just another example of what you can achieve with this machine by just applying some creativity. Since the Explore Air 2 can print then cut, you can create all sorts of business and planning supplies, like stickers and specialized note pads. Of course, the quality and success of your craftwork will depend on how you use your creativity and the types of materials and designs you choose.

To sum it all up, the Cricut Explore Air 2 has significant possibilities regarding material choice but also some limitations. Its main limitations consist of an inability to cut sturdy and extremely soft materials, which prevents you from using fabrics and wood. If this is a dealbreaker for you, then you should consider upgrading to the Maker.

Cricut Maker

The Cricut Maker is the brand's most powerful die-cutter. You can use it to cut, write, and score the widest range of materials. If you are a serious crafter or wish to use the Maker for business purposes and to produce marketable products, this machine gives you the widest range of possibilities in terms of materials and functions. As long as your material is under 3.32 inches or 2.3mm thick, you can count on your machine's ability to work with it.

Here's a short overview of all the types of materials your Cricut Maker will be able to work with:

Paper/cardstock. Your Cricut Maker will be able to cut through regular and adhesive cardstock, as well as chipboard between 1.5 and 2mm thickness. You can use it to work with construction and copy paper, as well as flocked and flat cardboard. Flocked paper is also Maker-friendly, as well as embossed and paper foil. You can also use your Cricut for cutting poster boards, freezer paper, as well as glitter paper and cardstock. The Maker will work well with kraft board, board foil, and paper. Metallic materials are also in the range of the machine's cutting abilities, which include metallic paper, cardstock, and poster board. It will create wonderful results with paper boards, as well as pearl paper, cardstock, and photographic paper. You can also use your maker to cut poster boards and post-its, and you can work on numerous types of paper, like rice, scrapbook, shimmer, wax, and watercolor paper. Solid and white core cardstock are also in the game.

Vinyl. The Cricut Maker also works with vinyl, which is great for producing quality, durable graphics, signs, and labels. It will work on adhesive, chalkboard, holographic, and dry erase vinyl. If you're looking forward to making Christmas decorations or other kinds of shiny decorative pieces, it also works with glitter, glossy, matte, pearl, and shimmer vinyl. You can utilize the Cricut Maker to work on outdoor vinyl as well, and you can also use it on permanent, removable, printable, true brushed, and stencil vinyl. Given the variety of vinyl to choose from, be sure to pick the right type for your project.

Iron-on. The Cricut Maker works well with almost all types of iron-on materials, from glossy, glitter, flocked, and foiled, to express and holographic. You can also use it for pattern, printable, and SportFlexed iron-ons, and you can use neon, mosaic, and mash iron-on for some flashy designs.

Textile and fabrics. You can use your Cricut Maker on cotton, chiffon, canvas, burlap, cashmere, and other light fabrics. You can also utilize the machine to cut through thick fabrics like linen, faux or real leather and suede, duck cloth, flannel, knits, jute, jersey, denim, and fleece. If you're into making edgy-looking jewelry, you can also use your Cricut Maker to cut metallic leather. This machine will also cut through muslin, moleskin, polyester, oilcloth, and printable fabric. You can also count on the Maker to cut through gentle fabrics like silk and soft metallic leather, and it will also work well with tulle, terry cloth, tweed, wool felt, and velvet.

Specialty materials. Your Cricut Maker will successfully cut many adhesive materials like wood, foil, duct tape, and washi tape. You can use it to cut aluminum foil and sheets, as well as birch and basswood. You can use it to cut corrugated paper and corkboard, and it will also work well with craft foam. This Cricut wonder will work great with foil acetate and glitter foam and cut through metallic vellum and magnet sheets like it's no big deal. You can also use it to cut the embossable foil, plastic packaging, paint chips, as well as printable sticker paper and magnet sheets. But, the list doesn't end there. You can even cut through soda cans with your Cricut Maker, and you can use stencil material, shrink plastic, tissue, and tattoo paper, as well as transparency film to make amazing artwork. Last but not least, you can use your Maker to cut wrapping paper, wood veneer, window clings, and even washi sheets.

Cricut Joy

Although the smallest in dimensions and arguably the most limited when it comes to functions and operations, the Cricut Joy still has plenty to offer. Depending on your interests, it may or may not be suited for robust production or business purposes. Still, the brand made Joy quite valuable by coming up with close to a hundred different materials that can be used with this machine.

The material list may not be as essential to know compared to the limitations in mechanical operations, but it's still important to understand what types of materials you can use with the Joy. It's also important to consider that the manufacturer carries plenty of materials for the machine that can be used without a mat, and there are plenty of materials designed for it available all over the web.

Instead of just listing the types of materials that the Joy can work with, this book will list the types of projects you can make instead. It will also provide you with some suggestions for materials, tools, and supplies that you can use for the best results and quality.

So without further ado, here is a list of materials that you can use on and with the Cricut Joy:

Insert cards. The Cricut Joy can cut a variety of types of paper that you can use to make impressive cards.

Decals. You can use the Joy to make personalized decals for coffee mugs, wood signs, laptops, phone cases, water bottles, pantry jars, and much more using Cricut Joy specialty vinyl. This vinyl comes in up to 20-ft. long rolls, and in pretty much any color and finish. Aside from permanent, you can also use Joy's specialty vinyl for re-stickable decals. This means that you can design and cut different-colored vinyl in a variety of finishes to make decals that you can remove from the surface and use somewhere else when needed. Of course, these materials also come with the transfer tape, another useful tool that helps you transfer vinyl decals easily without damaging your print. All you need to do is bind the tape to the piece with a scraper, transfer it to exactly where you need it, and then remove the tape.

Art and scrapbooking. The Cricut Joy works with dozens of deluxe papers that also come in a variety of colors and finishes. You may not be able to print patterns, but you're offered pre-patterned sticker papers that you can easily cut into any shape you choose. The inability to print is certainly a limitation, but it's compensated by an abundance of patterns that are designed for this machine, which allow you to bring pretty much any creative idea to life.

Iron-on materials. Although your Cricut Joy won't let you cut fabrics, you can most certainly create decorated household decor, accessories, clothes, and linens. The iron-on vinyl and foils that are suitable for the Joy will be quite sufficient for any decorative project you set your mind to doing.

Infusible ink. If you don't feel like ironing designs onto clothes and household items, how about tattooing them? It may sound strange, but Cricut created a vinyl substitute that can infuse ink into your material so that there's no chance that the design will get damaged. How amazing is that? Of course, you're given more than enough patterns, colors, and finishes to choose from.

Pens. Although primarily made for cutting, the Cricut Joy is also able to write and gives you the option to detach the blade and attach a pen in its place. Of course, the brand also came up with a dozen different pens, markers, and embellishments that will make any text look like it has been handwritten. Even better, this machine carries infusible ink pens that you can use on paper and fabric, which greatly expands your artistic possibilities.

You now know which materials to use with your selected Cricut. As you can see, whichever model you choose, there are plenty of options for you to make any project you want. Usually, people are most concerned about the inability of the cheaper models to create more robust or refined projects. Remember, there are always alternatives when it comes to materials.

For instance, if you want to make a large, sturdy quote decoration with your Cricut Joy, you can most certainly do it. How? Well, since you can't cut wood, you can cut multiple layers of chipboard and glue two or three pieces of the same cut one over the other. This way, you can achieve the sturdiness of basswood, for example, while still using the most ideal materials for your machine.

Or, you might feel discouraged if a machine within your budget range can't engrave or emboss. In this case, there is a life-saving hack. Here it is: You can cut as-thin-as-possible adhesive and iron-on vinyl and foil, and then apply them to leather notebooks or wallets and even acrylic blanks or metal jewelry like pendants to achieve the effect of engraving and embossing. The world is your oyster when it comes to finding workarounds and alternatives.

Chapter 7:

Creative Project Ideas – Easy and Intermediate

Now that you know the basics of using a Cricut machine, let's start making some amazing projects, shall we? We'll begin with easy- and beginner-friendly ideas for you to get some practice and inspiration. The following projects are best done on the Cricut Maker, but you'll be able to adjust them for other models as well.

Basswood Quote With Vinyl Highlights

https://pixabay.com/photos/conceptual-wooden-decorative-letters-1280533/

This fun project will look complex and intricate when finished, but making it will be easier than you could ever imagine! First things first, you'll need your Cricut Maker or Explore for the original project, and you can use substitute materials and slightly alter the design for a similar result with the Cricut Joy. Basswood decorations made with Cricut can be hung on a wall, displayed on a shelf, or placed on your coffee table next to a candle. They add warmth and style to your ambiance and, of course, give you an opportunity to share your thoughts and display them in your personal space.

https://pixabay.com/photos/message-quote-wood-flowers-petals-5451796/

Here's what you'll need for this project:

1. Transfer tape
2. One sheet of vinyl in the color and finish of your choosing
3. A plate of basswood, balsa wood, or a chipboard

And that's it!

Here's how to make your first beautiful project with Cricut. First, you will choose and design a quote. Open a worksheet (a Canvas) in Design Space, and set it up to present the size of your text box or a quote that's going to be cut. You can choose a phrase from the software's library, or you can open a text box and write one on your own. Next, position the text box on the Canvas and adjust font, style, and size.

The designing process is now over, and all you need to figure out is whether you wish to cover the entire quote with vinyl or use it only in certain layers (lines or parts of lines) to create highlights or accents. If you're confident in your layering skills, you can first start by cutting the quote on your wooden plate, and then go back to edit the project. Now, you'll choose only certain layers (lines) to cut from vinyl.

If you don't wish to do the project this way, you can instead cut an entire phrase in vinyl and apply it to the wood. You'll do this simply by keeping the design and changing the material settings. If you don't want to cover the whole quote with vinyl, you can select only certain letters (e.g., first and last, or every other) to still have some contrast with your design.

Finally, print the vinyl layers.

Once you've cut both wood and vinyl, it's time to transfer the vinyl design. Use transfer tape to lift the cut-out from the vinyl sheet, and apply it to the designated spot on your wooden cut-out. Repeat this process until you've set all the pieces into place, and your wonderful design is finished.

A Flower Corsage

https://pixabay.com/photos/prom-school-teen-dress-girl-4087893/

Whether for prom or Mother's Day, this project can be made in five easy steps and be a great present for a loved one in your family. If you're making a corsage for prom, make sure to match the colors of the flower to the colors of the dress. When you look at the picture, the design may appear to be more complex than it actually is. Don't let this intimidate you; the steps for making this project are easy and simple. The more time you spend making corsage flowers, the easier it will get. Plus, these are reusable and will last you multiple years.

For this project, you'll need cardstock, ribbons, pins, scissors, and glue. Let's go over the basic steps for the project:

1. Choose a flower template, and print it onto the cardstock.
2. Spray the cardstock, and curl the paper into the shapes you'd like. Adding moisture to the paper will help you create the desired shape.

3. Start gluing the flower together. Join tabs of each section, add leaves, and let the flower dry. To further set and secure the flower, use a clothespin to hold the flower's ends together while they're drying.

4. If you want to make your flower more colorful, add some color using markers or watercolors. Finally, glue the remaining parts of the flower together and let it dry.

5. Next, start making the ribbon. Cut a piece of ribbon in the desired length, and glue it to the flower once it's fully dry. You can further secure it with a pin.

If you have young children, you can make a Cricut corsage as a family project. You could involve the children in painting and gluing the flower and, depending on their age, you can also let them choose and cut ribbons.

Cricut Burlap Wreaths

Now, let's make a simple, neutral-looking burlap wreath that you can decorate with themed pins, badges, or stickers whenever you want to change up your decoration. You'll make a base for the burlap wreath on your Cricut, after which you can add holiday or season-themed decorations. If you're looking to commercialize your Cricut craft, you can easily create the burlap, add a couple of sets of embellishments for different seasons and holidays, and sell your product.

For this project, you should first choose the desired theme and the color scheme of your decoration. Keep in mind that burlap will be the best cut on the Cricut Maker, but you can choose an alternative material for your Explore or Joy. You should also choose the style of embellishments you wish to use, which you can get from any store. To further embellish your wreath, you can use different types of colored paper and cut them into various shapes such as snowflakes, leaves, hearts, or flowers—the choice is all yours.

Now, let's start making your all-in-on burlap Cricut wreath, shall we? Here's what you'll need for your project:

1. A wreath, which you can get made from foam, straw, or even cardstock.

2. One burlap ribbon. If you wish to switch the style and embellishments of your wreath, I recommend choosing a neutral-colored ribbon. Beige, gray, brown, or even deep red, green, or powder-rose will work. If you want the wreath to be an accent piece, you can also choose a silver or a golden ribbon. These are also neutral, will work with most of the embellishments, and should flatter a variety of wall paints and interior styles. The color of the burlap should also complement your interior design and contrast the color of your walls.

3. Printable embellishments. For this project, you can choose to focus on a single theme or cut multiple-themed embellishments from the start. I recommend looking for basic, neutral shapes and designs that are premade in your Design Space, cutting a few for testing purposes, and then choosing the ones that work best with your paper and burlap.

4. Sewing pins

5. Glue

Now, let's start making your burlap wreath. First, wrap the burlap around the wreath base and set it with glue and/or pins.

Start printing and cutting your embellishments. Given that you'll use a larger number of smaller embellishments, you can either design each individual embellishments or find a suitable printable pattern, print it, and cut out the desired shapes manually.

Attach the embellishments to the ribbon of your wreath, and you're done. As you can see, the larger portion of this project consists of printing and cutting your embellishments. The very basic way to do this project would be to just cut interesting shapes out of colored paper, metallic paper, crepe paper, or any other type of paper that works with the style you choose.

If you wish to add complexity and quality to your project, you can first write notes or draw pictures on the desired shapes and even apply some embossing or scoring to add flair and texture. It all depends on the machine you have, your style, taste, and, of course, creativity.

Easy Cricut Stamps

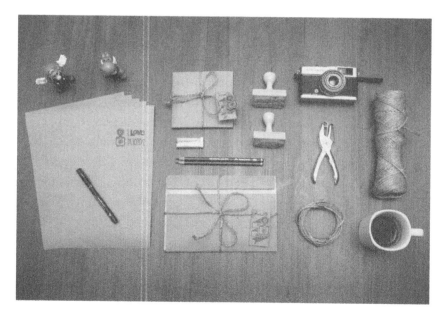

https://pixabay.com/photos/background-photos-photography-paper-1209461/

Stamps are among the easiest projects to make with a Cricut machine. You can choose the sturdiest material that works with your Cricut, but it will ideally be foam and basswood for the best quality result.

This tutorial will demonstrate making stamps by first cutting a basswood base and then creating shapes from craft foam. Keep in mind that these are also the most expensive materials. If you wish to choose something more budget-friendly, you can cut stamp handles from cardstock or chipboard, then hand-cut pieces of other material that you wish to use. Remember to only use material sheets that are suitable for your Cricut model since they will come in the best dimensions to work with your specific blade.

For this project, you'll need the following items:

1. Stamp designs. Given that this tutorial uses craft foam, understand that the material may not work well with intricate designs. If you're a beginner, choose simple designs like basic animal shapes, geometric shapes, hearts, flowers, stars, and others that don't require cutting very thin lines. Choosing simpler shapes will also speed up the process since your cutter won't have to take extra time to cut smaller chunks of material.

2. Craft foam sheets. You will ideally create a project sheet with matching stamp shapes that are aligned in such a way to use most of the material. For this project, you'll need a single canvas scheme that you can cut onto a cording foam sheet, and repeat the process for as many sheets as you'd like. The color of the foam won't affect the color of the stamp, so you can choose whichever you like as long as it's made for your specific Cricut.

3. Basswood boards. This project will use basswood boards as one of the sturdiest materials, but you can choose any sturdy alternative you like that works with your Cricut. Cardstock, chipboard, or balsa wood are all suitable alternatives.

4. Glue. You need a powerful glue for your project, so hot glue or your favorite craft glue will work the best.
5. Stamp ink, which you can get in a variety of colors.

Now, let's start making your stamps. The first step is to design and save your shapes. Create two different boards, one featuring your stamp shapes that will be cut on craft foam and the other for stamp bases/handles. Create a pattern of shapes for your stamp base and the handle side by side for material preservation.

To design a handle, I recommend using a simple geometric shape like a square or a rectangle with a length that matches either height or length of your base shape (whichever is shorter). This way, you'll easily align the shapes for printing, speed up the process, and use up the maximum material. Make sure that the number of stamp designs matches the number of bases and handles.

Now, onto the cutting. You can easily fit ten different stamp shapes onto a single craft foam sheet, so start by cutting those shapes. Next, cut your base and handle parts. When you're working with hard materials, it is possible that the pieces won't be fully cut from the board. Prepare a scalpel or a knife to gently separate pieces and remove them from the board after you've first peeled them off the mat.

The only remaining step is to glue foam stamps to their bases, leave them to dry, and then add handles. And voila, you're done!

From my experience, this project shouldn't take longer than two hours. What I particularly like about making stamps with the Cricut is that they're commercial-friendly, meaning that you can make a decent amount of them in a single day and also sell them for a good price. If you're making the project for your own pleasure, you can make adorable stamps for your kids or even some for your own purposes.

Cricut Iron-On Pillowcases and Linens

Did you know that you can personalize sheets, pillowcases, and other linens in under an hour using the Cricut? Whether you want to make your own bedding look special or give a personalized present to a friend or a family member, this technique could be a great way to express your sentiment.

Here's what you'll need for this project:

1. Iron-on foil sheets. Pick any type of iron-on foil that you like, as long as it's made for your Cricut model.
2. A set of linens. Sheets, pillowcases, and other items that you wish to personalize should be washed and ironed prior to transferring the vinyl designs.
3. An iron or a hot press. Your design will be transferred using heat, so you need either an iron or a hot press to do this.
4. A design. You can either create your own designs in Design Space or open one of the pre-made projects that come with the software. When cutting iron-on designs, whether it's foil or vinyl, you need to "mirror" the design before cutting. In other words, choose the "mirror" option in your Design Space, and it will create a mirror image of your print. You need to do this because when cutting any iron-on, it needs to be done with the foil, or vinyl side, down (facing the mat) so that the backside of the material faces the knife. This is necessary due to the technique you're using to transfer the material; you need to keep the translucent layer over the foil for transferring purposes.

As you can probably tell, this process is quite straightforward, but let's lay out the main steps just in case:

1. First, you need to pick a design and cut it using your Cricut. Make sure to load the material right-side-down for an easier transfer, and to mirror the image in Design Space before cutting.
2. Next, you need to unload the Cricut and gently remove excess foil, but without damaging the top translucent layer of foil. This foil will serve for safe and easy transferring, so you want to keep that top layer whole, without cuts or gaps.
3. Place your pillowcase on the iron board and iron over the spot that's designated for placing the print.
4. Gently lay the print on the pillowcase, this time with the right side up. You will see the cut-out print that's covered with a translucent layer of foil. Once you set your print, you'll notice that the foil has stuck at the fabric lightly. This is why it's important to be patient and precise.
5. Cover the design with another piece of fabric with a thickness of light-to-medium, or a cloth. Iron over it for a minute or two. Remove the transfer foil after it's cooled down enough to be safe to touch.

You're done! You now have a fully personalized pillowcase. You can use the same steps to apply vinyl or foil prints on any other piece of fabric, including sheets, tablecloths, or T-shirts. The quality of your work will largely depend on the quality of your print. Also, not all materials can bear frequent handling and washing. Before choosing your foils and vinyls, check if they're machine-washable, and also read the reviews to see how they handle being washed, how long they last, and whether or not they're prone to peeling and cracking.

Now that you're gaining more experience, let's start making a bit more complex projects. The next chapter will show you how to create more advanced craftwork with your Cricut machine.

Chapter 8:

Creative Project Ideas – Advanced and Marketable

Is there truly a complex project with Cricut? After spending some time working with the machine, I realized that it's only the result that may come across as difficult. Essentially, Cricut's functions are vital to understand. Advanced skills pretty much include learning how to combine them in a smart, creative way to achieve what appears to be unachievable. Of course, careful planning is necessary for your craftwork to turn out the way you want.

Some projects that we'll make in this chapter seem complex to create because the cuts turn out to be larger than the Cricut mat, combine multiple printing layers, or require working on sturdier materials, like the acrylic. Indeed, these projects will require advanced skills in designing and cutting, but making them doesn't have to be difficult. As long as you follow the given instruction, you'll have a great time playing with your Cricut!

A Large 3D Cricut Shadowbox

How about making a 3D lighted shadow box? These projects might look difficult to create, but it's far easier than you might think. When making this design, you will apply the technique known as layering. Essentially, you will choose an image or a figure, then cut it in such a way as to separate layers of lines and elements to create depth.

For this project, you'll need:

1. Three to five paper sheets
2. A lightbox
3. Hot glue
4. A sheet of craft foam

Now, let's start making your 3D box. Here are the steps that you need to follow:

1. The first step is to create your design in Design Space. Start by making a square shape in the size of your shadowbox. This will be the frame for your drawing. Build the image from the back to forward in layers, which creates the 3D effect.

2. When making your drawing, first add the background, then the furthest elements of the drawing, like houses, trees, etc. Finally, apply the last layer, which contains the elements of the drawing that are the closest to the eye. This form of layering creates an illusion of depth in the cut after you apply one sheet of paper over the other. However, each of the elements should touch the surface of the square; the layers shouldn't overlap.

3. Measure the inside of your box to double-check the dimensions and click "Make it". You will cut the layers sheet by sheet, starting from the final layer and moving toward the first one on your design. Since you'll be cutting a complex image, some of the smaller pieces of paper might get stuck to the mat. Make sure to remove them regularly before starting a second cut. Also, look at the images on your Design Space frequently to remind yourself of what each layer is supposed to look like. Since you're not printing a complex drawing on a single sheet of paper but instead creating a complex image out of multiple sheets of paper, you might get lost in all the shapes and lines.

4. Now that you've cut all the layers, cut thin strips of craft foam to create the "spacers" for your project. You will create a type

of foam frame for each of the layers which separate one from the next. Make sure that the foam is at the edge of your paper, and glue the foam strips over the four back edges of your sheet. This means gluing while the paper is turned upside-down. Repeat these steps on all layers of paper, and apply each of them right-side-up, one on top of the other, into the box and over the lights. Once you're finished layering, apply the lid. The lid will keep the layers fixed.

If you followed all of the steps, you now have a whimsical-looking shadow box that will look wonderful in your or your child's bedroom. I advise getting a high-quality lightbox, because disassembling the entire piece if the lights break down might damage the design, aside from being a real hassle. If you don't want to purchase a lightbox, you can use a thick, deeper picture frame you already have and only get adhesive lights. Fix the lights to the inner edges of the frame, and you're finished. In this case, make sure to drill a hole in the bottom corner of the frame for the cord to pass through.

Engraved Jewelry With Cricut

https://pixabay.com/photos/pendant-gold-medallion-jewelry-939194/

Let's make an engraved charm bracelet!

For this project, you will be using Cricut's engraving tool. You will purchase jewelry pieces for your bracelet, then use the Cricut to add intricate engravings that will give them extra value. For this project, I recommend investing in a stainless steel charm bracelet. Get a bracelet with multiple plates in different shapes and sizes.

You will need:

1. The Cricut engraving tool, which has a sharp point that applies pressure to inscribe words and images into plastic, leather, paper, acrylic, and soft metal materials. It is best used on the Cricut Maker, which features the Adaptive Tool System. This system applies the necessary amount of pressure that's needed for engraving. You will not be able to use this tool on the Cricut Explore Air or the Cricut Joy.
2. Stainless steel plates in the desired shape and size
3. A design for your engraving
4. A chain bracelet
5. A pair of pliers

Now, let's start making your engraved charm bracelet. Here are the steps for carrying out this project:

1. Start designing your engravings. This process begins by creating templates for your charms and making sure that you're designing for the unique size of each plate. To start designing your engraved charmed plates, open a new Canvas in your Design Space, upload the desired image, or write the text. If you choose a design with thicker lines, you're going to have to fill it with close-together lines. This way, the tool will create multiple thin lines within the selected spaces to create a filling effect.
2. Choose quotes, text, or images that you wish to apply to your plate, and then apply them onto the base shape of your plates.

Pay attention to size, legibility, alignment, and the positioning of your engravings. Take your time with this step, and carefully adjust each image, letter, or pattern, because you won't be able to correct them later on.

3. To engrave both the front and the back, you need to separate the work onto two different mats and center the positioning of the design in the exact place where you'll place the plates for the charm bracelet.

4. Next, lay the plates on the designated spots on the mat, and set them with tape. Don't worry, your engraving tool will work well over the tape and won't compromise the design. Don't forget to set up the machine for engraving and to select the correct material for it to apply the right amount of speed and pressure.

5. Load the mat into the machine, press "Make it" in your Design Space, and watch the beauty unfold!

6. After clicking "Make it", the software will guide you to place the tool in the Maker's carrier.

7. If you wish to engrave both sides off the plate, you're going to have to repeat the process for the other side. This means that you'll need to unload the mat, remove the plates, switch sides, and still make sure that they're fixed in the exact spots as previously.

And that's it. With some careful planning and designing, you have a wonderful, unique bracelet that you can keep for yourself or give to someone you love!

Cricut 3D Decorations

https://pixabay.com/illustrations/framed-digital-paper-shadowbox-5250516/

Now, let's make a multilayered cardstock decoration. Cardstock may seem like cheap paper, but if you use it the right way, you can create elegant-looking designs. Layering is a technique that requires more planning and technical skill, but it adds value to your creation. For this project, you'll need multiple sheets of different-colored cardstock paper.

Next, you need to find a 3D layered design that you wish to print. There are plenty of both free and paid designs that you can browse through. The design information will also tell you how many layers there are. You can choose whether to print multiple layers on a single sheet of paper or to enlarge a design and print it over the entire paper sheet.

Here are the steps for making this project:

1. Load your layered design into the Design Space, and open the images on a new Canvas. You'll see all of the layers at the top

right corner of the screen. Once you click "group", you'll be able to adjust the size for the entire piece.

2. Next, choose the preferred placement of the design on the mat and ungroup the layers. Click "Make it", and start loading the paper and cutting. You'll have to cut each individual layer, then glue one layer over the other while making sure that you're arranging the layers in the right order.

3. Leave the finished piece to dry, and you're done.

Here are a couple of tips to keep in mind when cutting layered decorations:

*   Check material settings. Intricate patterns and shapes may not come out well on thicker materials like cardstock. Make sure to check whether the design mentioned the preferred materials to use. If you like a design that will not work with your desired material, you can somewhat compensate by enlarging the design. This will result in a bigger piece but also a better cutting accuracy.

*   Be careful with the glue. The more intricate your design is, the more accuracy you'll need when it comes to gluing. If you're working with paper, utilize paper glue, applying it slowly and gently across the surface of a layer.

*   To avoid using too much glue, start applying it from the back of the top layer since top layers are almost always the smallest in size. Finish by gluing the front end of the bottom layer, which is usually the thickest and largest.

*   If this is your first time making a layered project, I recommend using a pre-made design to see how the cutting works. After you become used to cutting and making designs like these, you can move on to drawing your designs either on a computer or even by hand, then scanning them for cutting and printing.

You can use this technique to make beautiful Christmas ornaments, jewelry like pendants, earrings, and bracelets, and more. You can even utilize this technique to cut layers of fabrics and create elegant, rustic designs.

A 3D Acrylic Engraved Lamp

The previous section showed you how to engrave, and the one before demonstrated how to create a realistic-looking shadowbox. So, why not combine the two and create a high-value decorative lamp? Given the amount of skill, quality, and effort involved in making this product, it would be a worthy present for a housewarming party, baby shower, a wedding, or any other important occasion. You can even market it for a high price once you polish your skills and gain more creativity. Once you're finished making it, you will be amazed by its depth, complexity, and warmth.

What you'll essentially do to create this lamp is use the layering technique to create an intricate design on multiple acrylic blanks, then apply it using engravement for an extra refined look. If you don't have an engraving tool, or if your Cricut doesn't support this function, you can substitute engraving by using adhesive foil to print your layers. With this technique, you can also combine different colors. My style recommendation would be to choose light, pastel colors that only slightly contrast one another for the best result.

Now, onto our project. Here are the supplies you'll need:
1. A light shadowbox
2. Multiple acrylic blank plates
3. A layered design of your choice
4. A sheet of paper foam
5. Multiple sheets of adhesive foil if you're working with the Cricut Explore or the Cricut Joy

Let's start making your awesome 3D engraved acrylic lamp. Here are the steps:

1. Load your design into a new Canvas, and then separate it into different layers per instructions given in the first project. Don't forget to set your material settings to acrylic so that your machine can set up the right engraving speed and pressure, and also set up your Linetype to Engrave. When you click Linetype, a drop-down box will show a list of functions, and all you need to do is select Engrave. (If you're working with a Cricut Explore, you'll do this slightly differently; you will set the material to adhesive foil, and then set Linetype to Cut.) Once your design is properly centered and sized, all you need to do is click 'Make it' and let the party begin.

2. The machine will guide you to load the acrylic, or foil, and apply one layer after another. If you're using the engraving tool, the software will remind you to attach it. You will need the Quick Swap housing for this tool, which you'll most likely get with one of the many tools that come with the machine. After each of the layers is finished, the software will prompt you to insert another sheet of material.

3. If you're working with a Maker, your plates will be ready after the final layer is engraved. If you're working with an Explore or Joy, you will have multiple sheets of foil to transfer onto the acrylic plates. Start by removing the excess foil and keeping the translucent top layer, which will make the transfer easier. Make sure that your foil is well-aligned so that all of the layers on individual acrylic plates work well together.

4. Once your plates are finished, you now need to cut the right-sized pieces of craft foam as instructed in the first project and glue it along the edges of the plates. Give the plates some time to dry, then layer them starting from the back layer all the way to the front. Close your lightbox, turn the lights on, and admire your creation! Your design will look like it took ages to make,

and only you will know how easy and fun it was to actually do it.

These layered 3D designs can do wonders for the ambiance of a room. You can choose a nice aquarium design for your bedroom or a winter landscape for the living room. Either way, the effect that will be created once you turn on the lights will leave anyone speechless.

Layered Multicolor Vinyl Stickers

You've come so far. If you haven't made any of the projects yet, you're most certainly equipped to do it. I'll now show you how to make a seemingly simple but still complex project. You will learn how to make layered vinyl stickers, which will help you create lively, colorful stickers that have both a heartwarming effect and the potential for sales.

Here's what you'll need for this:

1. Multiple vinyl sheets in different colors, depending on the colors of your image
2. A vinyl scraper
3. Transfer tape
4. A layered image design
5. A pair of scissors. To make layering the material easier and preserve vinyl, you can cut around the layer before removing the excess vinyl.

https://pixabay.com/illustrations/hearts-puffy-shiny-love-sticker-4299927/

Are you ready? Let's start making our last complex project! For this one, I recommend finding a simple image of an animal with a maximum of three different colors. Take a look at those colors and set aside the coordinating vinyl sheets.

Now, let's overview the basic steps. Upload a layered image. Count the colors and choose "complex". Now, start selecting layers. Start with the color that's the least present in the drawing and keep it, erasing everything else. If you're cutting a cat, it will most likely be paws, ears, eyes, and nose in the darkest color. Make sure that there are no lines left after you're done erasing other colors. Once you're done cleaning the layer, click "continue" and save the cut file. Make sure to name it recognizably to know which layer it represents. Remember to save each image as a "cut" file.

Again, load the whole image, select the second color, and erase all other elements. If you're working on our cat sample, it will most likely be a lighter color on its belly, stripes on the tale, or freckles on its head and paws. Repeat the steps of saving the layer as a "cut" file.

Finally, finish with a dominating color. If you're not cutting a black cat, it will most likely be the color of its fur that extends from the top of its head to its legs and tail. Erase all other colors from the original picture except that one, and save the image as the "cut" file.

Once you're done making all the layers, it's time to open a new Canvas and add all of the cut files, this time in reverse order from the one you created them in. You'll most likely have anywhere from three to five different layers. Load them all to the Canvas and change the color of the layer to match the color of the material. This way, it will be a lot easier to identify the exact sheets to use. Align all layers, adjust the size on the sheet, and click "Make it".

Your Cricut will now start each of the laters, prompting you to load the right-colored sheet when needed. Since vinyl sheets take a little bit of time to clean up and weed, you should start removing the excess material from the first sheet right after you're done loading the second one. By the time you're finished, you will have prepared all the layers for finalizing the sticker. Once you prepare the last one by removing the excess material and weeding, you can start layering your sticker.

To do this, apply a piece of transfer tape onto the first cut-out. Scrape over it with the Cricut's vinyl scraper gently to make sure that all the material has adhered to the tape, then lift it from its base. Now comes the part where you need to be really precise, patient, and careful. Going in the exact order in which the layer was printed, continue applying one cut-out layer after another to the adhesive side of the transfer tape.

Once you have positioned a cut-out correctly, scrape over the transfer tape gently, and lift the vinyl from its base. After you've finished the last layer, your sticker is now complete. It's time to transfer it onto its designated surface.

These types of stickers require some additional work, but they have more depth and dimension compared to the single-layer ones. You can decide whether to transfer your sticker onto a mug, a baby bottle, a mason jar, or anywhere else you'd like. The quality of the sticker will depend on the material, and you can make your sticker dishwasher-safe by applying specialty sealers. I'll leave the choice of the brand up to you, but I believe the best quality ones are worthy of the investment.

Now, let's talk about the commercial potential that these little stickers have. You can sell mugs, bottles, and other personalized items, even the highly marketable baby cups and bottles. You can even start your own little service where your customers can be allowed to choose a print that will be put on their items. Learning how to create layered projects and cut files is the most complicated part of the process, but it is definitely worth it.

You're all set now. If you made at least a couple of these projects, you're probably familiarized with the machine, as well as with your creative affinities and inspiration. You've most likely found something that moves you, so why not take your craft a step further?

The next chapter will show you how to start making money with your Cricut. You will learn the basics of production, calculating profits, costs, and prices, and so much more!

Chapter 9:

How to Monetize Cricut

Now that you learned how to make complex projects with your Cricut, why not consider starting a business? After all, home-based crafting businesses are grossing billions of dollars yearly nationwide. As it turns out, planning your business the right way can result in thousands of dollars of profit within three months. However, it will take careful planning and patience, and your success won't happen overnight. In this chapter, we will go over some basic steps for running a successful business with your Cricut.

https://pixabay.com/photos/home-office-apple-inc-business-569359/

Design a Unique Product

When working with a Cricut, you have the advantage of being able to design every single aspect of your creation, from the product itself to add-ons and the packaging. However, the trick is in standing out. Nowadays, people can get anything and everything for cheap, but quality and authenticity cost. Uniqueness always had value in the market, meaning that you will have to come up with a line of products like no other. The best way to do this is simply to draw from your own uniqueness and the quirky side of your personality.

Remember, your buyers will be a lot like you. They will be men and women who appreciate aesthetics, quality, uniqueness, and creativity. They are constantly on the lookout for a product that no one else has, and you're the right person to give them that!

There's a whole community of Cricut crafters out there, and you can easily become one of the players if you bring all of your unique creativity to light. Think about a Cricut-made product that serves the most purpose to you—the one you're making for yourself over and over again,—and redesign it to add your special flair.

Boost Your Skills

Now, having an amazing business idea is one thing, but actually putting it in motion is a completely different story. Before you invest in materials and marketing, make sure that your Cricut skills match your goals. With so many different functions, there are no limits to the types of products and effects you can create with your imagination.

As you have probably noticed by now, a single result can be achieved with Cricut in many different ways, all of which affect how long it will take to produce and distribute your product. Experiment with different applications and techniques to find the most innovative yet economic way to create your project. Of course, make sure to add your own spin on it to maximize your profits.

Also, don't be afraid to invest! The more you improve your supplies in terms of designs, fonts, and the variety of offerings, the better the chances of succeeding. You can always find numerous freebies, coupons, and affordable designs across the web.

You most likely have dozens of product ideas up your sleeve. However, you'll have to narrow down your offers so that you know what to focus on. If you become known for a particular line of products, you will form a steady stream of customers. So, whether you choose shirts, paper flowers, or jewelry, stick to that particular group of products.

You might feel like catering to everyone will grow your business, but this isn't true. If you follow this path, you'll most likely end up not catering to anyone and without a memorable product that people will associate with your name. It might also result in major money loss since you'll be spending a lot of energy and resources for a small number of sales that most likely won't result in repeated shoppers. Instead of trying to please everyone, stick to one particular group of products, and continue investing in that line while building up your skills.

Consistency

Once you start with your Cricut business, make sure to be consistent and work on it each day. It may not have to be the production; instead, you can think about other aspects of your business, like marketing and budgeting. Make a daily schedule of what you need to do to grow your business and stick to it. Aside from this, consistency in price and quality is important as well.

As soon as you put out a product within a certain price category, you'll attract a particular consumer base whose budget fits your pricing. If you switch price categories, you might lose that customer base. Your customers will also expect a certain level of quality, so make sure to measure up to their expectations with each purchase.

Have a Business Strategy

Although creative in nature, running a business with Cricut is still a business. Don't shy away from consulting tax advisors, accountants, attending entrepreneurship, business classes, and webinars, and doing everything else you can to become a wise business person. If your business kicks off, you will find yourself in the shoes of a CEO with much to gain and much to lose.

Remember, companies that have a background rarely fail because of their products. They usually fail because of mismanagement of the business. It happens when a business cuts back on quality for the sake of profit, taking up more work than they can handle, getting higher loans than they can pay off, failing to adjust to changing business climates, and other business-related reasons.

https://pixabay.com/photos/man-work-desk-business-person-597178/

Set Realistic Cricut Goals

The best-led business is goal-driven, and you can write a perfectly fine business plan and advertising strategy that revolves around goals with a little under a month of research and calculation. You can gain precious knowledge by simply visiting Google Scholar and reading studies on the most popular and most profitable products, leadership styles, business practices, and marketing strategies. This work will pay off as you'll be able to quite accurately calculate how much you can charge for your product and how this number fits into your business and personal financial plan.

On that note, don't be afraid to set the lowest possible goals. Even if you aim to profit half of your town's average minimum wage and manage to achieve this, you're better off facing initial success than feeling like you're failing from the get-go. On the other hand, make sure that you're not losing money or underpricing your product.

Do Your Math

Once you start marketing your products, the price must compensate for all of your supplies, production costs, taxes, utility costs, and, of course, your time. It may appear as if you should start with a low price to gain momentum, but once your customers get used to low prices, it will be hard to convince them that the product is worth more later on. If you don't feel like doing all of these complex calculations, rely on the common rule that your selling price should be between the doubled and quadrupled supply cost.

Of course, small tweaks and adjustments can make a difference to consumers, so make sure to adjust your price further by looking into competitive products. As a new seller, you should be slightly more affordable than the competition, but not too much. If you price your product too low, you risk being perceived as a low-quality brand.

https://pixabay.com/illustrations/woman-laptop-notebook-sitting-1459220/

Accent Quality

Regardless of your product category, maximize the quality of your product by investing in quality materials and your skills. If needed, you can try to lower the price by figuring out more practical steps to design your product. As mentioned earlier, there are multiple ways to achieve the same result with Cricut, and you should try to adjust the process so that it becomes more efficient. Furthermore, you should adjust product sizes to reduce material waste, which will result in material savings.

Cent by cent, small adjustments made in planning and production can, indeed, lower the price of your product without compromising quality and profitability. Whenever you feel like you need to cut costs, first look into ways to make your work more practical and time-efficient, and only if necessary, consider using cheaper materials, cutting back on the product size, etc.

https://pixabay.com/illustrations/devops-business-process-improvement-3148393/

Offer Customization

If you designed a line of profitable products, you can further maximize your income by adding different customization options that work with your financial and business concept. For example, if you're selling products with text written on them, offer your consumers an opportunity to choose the text color, font, or even the text itself.

Of course, don't forget to charge as much as needed to compensate for the extra work. Add at least 20% to the original product price, considering that you'll have to take at least 30 minutes of your time to add the clients desired adjustments, unlike with uniform products where you can open a design and start printing and cutting without having to give attention to individual pieces.

Run a Quality Control Check

You have a top-notch machine, you have premium quality materials, and you've put a ton of work into creating authentic designs. So, what could go wrong? Well, it could happen that you develop your business, buy ten Makers, connect them to your laptop, and start producing hundreds or even thousands of products each day. Let's say that there's a flaw in a batch of materials you purchased or an error in your design (e.g., misaligned text, the wrong font, a typo, etc.).

Unless you're careful, you could end up sending hundreds of faulty packages, being swamped with refund requests, and having your store's social media blasted with poor reviews. So, how do you prevent this from happening? The answer is by having a steady quality control routine.

Quality control is done simply, by pulling out and checking one out of each class, category, or batch of products and making sure that it meets your quality standards. That way, even if some of the faulty products do reach your customers, it won't become a massive issue. It will be an isolated mishap that you'll be able to "iron out" easily.

Chapter 10:

Cricut Tips, Tricks, and Hacks

Great job! You're almost through this book, and you're close to understanding everything you need to know about using Cricut cutters, creating amazing craftwork, and profiting with it. These final pages will let you in on useful little hacks that you can use with your Cricut to maximize material use, make creation easier, and save time. Here's what you can do to hack your way to seamless Cricut art...

Careful Peeling

When you're done cutting your materials, you are supposed to separate the material from the mat. Most people instinctively peel away the material from the mat. However, whether it's vinyl, cardstock, or adhesive paper, doing so comes at the risk of damaging or tearing your material. What you should do instead is curl the mat and peel it away from the material. Simply reverse the common step, and you'll preserve a lot more material than you otherwise would.

If you start creating products in bulk, you'll likely have quite a speedy production routine. Using this hack will assure that you reduce material waste and have more quality products to market.

Careful Vinyl Storage

Storing rolls of vinyl can consume both space and time. If you don't have a good system, you could be spending hours each day rolling through different types of vinyl while you're trying to find the right one. Instead of having to look through dozens of different vinyl rolls each day, you can simply sort them in IKE bag storage holders. These convenient storage holders will allow you to sort your vinyl by color, type, or any other way you choose, and make it easier to look through the rolls while you're working.

Keep Your Blade Sharp

Did you know that there is an easy way to sharpen your Cricut blade? All you need to do is use a piece of tin foil. Remove the blade from its clamp, and run it through the tin foil between 10 and 12 times. This trick can significantly extend your blade's shelf life.

Organize Your Cricket Blades

In case you didn't notice, your Cricut has a place for you to store all of its add-on tools and small plates. You can safely store all the necessary tools and add-ons inside your machine when you're not using it. However, before you start using your Cricut again, make sure that there are no leftover tools that might intervene with the performance of the machine.

Easy Cleaning

Did you know that there is a simple and hassle-free way for you to clean glitter, paper, and vinyl scrap leftovers from your machine? It's true. All you need to do is run a lint roller through the side of your machine, and you will easily collect any small pieces of leftover materials. The same goes for your workspace.

Use Any Pen Brand You Want

If you don't want to use only Cricut's brand pens for your craftwork, the Explore Air 2 has an attachment that allows you to add any other pen to your machine. The best way to do this is to use a specially made pen adapter. With the Explore Air 2, you can find the adapters that will attach any other pan to your blade and ensure that it works well with the machine. This includes Sharpies, ink pens, and anything else you like. However, make sure to carefully read the instructions so that you attach the pen the right way.

The Vinyl Weeding Hack

Did you know that there is an easy and simple way to weed your vinyl scraps? All you need to do is get a nail polish holder, and store the vinyl scraps there. No more mess at your workspace, and no more having to figure out different ways to store and collect scraps of material.

Find Software Freebies

Of course, Cricuts come with a free Design Space installation. So, why would you want any other software? As it turns out, there are a couple of them out there that require a subscription, but they do make the design process considerably easier. The best part is that you can find coupons and discounts for these all over the internet.

Make sure to check out other apps as well to see if they have particular functions that would make your work easier. For example, some of them convert files effortlessly, while others let you design with more ease and convenience.

Store Supplies on a Pegboard

There are only a few types of boards that are as convenient as pegboards. These boards allow you to add hooks to them, then attach containers for any tools and supplies you need. This is a great way to organize, considering that these boards come at a fraction of the price you'd usually pay for an organizer. They have a couple of other advantages as well, though. They use up vertical wall space, meaning that no working space will be taken away from your office or workshop. Plus, they are highly adjustable, and you can move your containers around, add more, and remove them exactly as you need.

Easy Mat Cleaning

Cricut mats are simple to use, but they can pick up debris over time. Instead of throwing out your mat, you can effortlessly wipe it down with baby wipes, and then spray a couple of layers of adhesive spray on it. You can easily get up to ten uses out of your mat if you use this method.

Vinyl Hack #2: Slap Bracelets

Working with vinyl is amazing, but organizing it requires a bit more cunning. There's another cheap way to keep your vinyl rolls together. All you need to do is fix them with slap bracelets, and you're done.

Wood Bin Material Organization

Rolls and rolls of paper, adhesive, glitter foil, and other items can be a pain to organize. The fact that they can look very similar, and so it's possible to mix them up is one more reason to give your organizing habits more attention. So, what's another way to organize your rolls of paper, vinyl, and fabrics? The answer is wood bins! The process is easy. You need a number of bins to match the type of materials. Just label the bins, and your work is complete.

Cut Materials With Straight Edges

If you're using an off-brand material with your Cricut, you're going to have to adjust the dimensions of the machine. As a result of this, you might end up with plenty of material waste. One of the ways to prevent this is to trim the sheets before loading them into the machine by using a straight edge. Neat, right?

Use Free Digital Resources

Did you know that there are multiple websites out there that offer completely free images and vectors? Why shop for designs when you can download them for free? The same goes for patterns and quotes.

Fix Materials With Painter's Tape

Having your thick materials slide on the mat can be frustrating. Luckily, there's a simple way to deal with this problem, and it is to use painter's tape. This tape will damage neither the mat nor your material as it's made to be used on walls without ripping off their paint.

After you're done working on your project, you can just remove the tape, no flaws left behind. This hack is particularly great for wood and chipboard.

Use Transfer Tape for Neat Curved Surfaces

If you're looking for a way to keep your material smooth when making a curved surface, there's a very simple hack that you can use. What you need to do is cut slits around the edges of the transfer tape so that you can place the design with more accuracy. That way, there won't be any last-minute mess-ups just when you think you got your design right.

Write Down Your Cheats

Different materials on the Cricut require a different setting, adjustments, and add-ons when cutting, scoring, printing, and writing. If you want to work with a multitude of materials, and you don't want to get lost in the settings, print out your cheat sheet for the right add-ons and customizations for certain materials.

Chances are high that you won't be able to memorize all the functions, settings, and pathways for each of your projects. So, why not write or print out your cheat sheets? Having a reminder by your side will ensure that you won't get lost while you're trying to work on a project, and also that you won't set the wrong settings by accident. You can print your cheat sheet and keep it next to your laptop.

When planning a project as a beginner, it can also be useful to plan and write out your ideas for how creating the project is going to go, as well as the exact pathways in Design Space you'll use for the necessary settings. You can also write out which knives, pens, mats, and Design Space pathways to use when working on balsa wood, vinyl, paper, etc.

Use Magazine Holders

If you need to work on the go, and you require a limited number of materials for your project, it could be a good idea to store them in a magazine holder. This is an easy way to sort and carry your materials. You can either stack or roll the materials as needed, and you can also further adjust the organizer by adding dividers and labels. Magazine holders are yet another solution for material organizing without having to spend money on brand-new organizers.

Use Adhesives on Wood

There's nothing better than combining beauty with quality in your craftwork. Adhesive vinyl can give just the right tone and texture to your creation, and you can also use it for adhering images, patterns, and quotes to almost any wooden piece. Arguably, balsa wood is one of the sturdiest materials to work on with Cricut, so combining the two will result in the best combination of quality, sturdiness, and beauty.

You can use this combo on a multitude of projects and decorations, from pictures to lamps and even jewelry organizers. Don't forget to carefully choose the type of vinyl to combine with wood so that you don't end up with a cheap look.

Check Design Space for Freebies First

Do you need a new pattern or font? Make sure to check Design Space before purchasing anything to see if they have some freebies or discounts worthy of your attention. It may appear at times that those graphics you need to purchase are better quality compared to those that come for free, and you might be able to notice subtle differences from your end. But will other people be able to tell the difference, and will paying for a digital asset make any true difference to the quality of your products? Sometimes they will, but most of the time, there are perfectly fine freebies that you can download instead of paying. So, why pay when you don't have to?

Scour the Internet for Free Fonts

The more variety and uniqueness to your projects and products, the better. The moment you become a serious Cricut crafter, you'll start paying attention to the little things that make big differences in a product's value. Uniqueness will be one of those things, which is why you'll most likely want as many different fonts as possible. Don't forget that the web is swarming with free fonts that you can download in exchange for a subscription or by simply giving out your email. Don't miss out on these amazing opportunities!

Conclusion

You first learned what a Cricut die-cutter is. You learned that all Cricut die-cutters have the ability to cut out exact shapes and draw lines as dictated by their software, Design Space. Once you learned this, it was probably a novelty that Cricuts don't really print. All of the Cricut models can cut, write, and draw, but only some can also emboss, engrave, and score.

Moreover, you learned that the Cricut machines differ not only in the range of operations that they can perform, but also in the variety of materials they can work with. You also found out that die-cutters work by following the commands you set on your computer, including the exact design to cut, write, or draw. It was at that point, when you knew exactly what these Cricut machines do, that it was time to choose your favorite.

Upon learning the basic information about Cricut die-cutters, it was time to answer a second important question: What's the difference between the Maker, the Explore Air 2, and the Joy? Despite the obvious price variations, you were to find out the exact possibilities and functionalities of each Cricut model, so that you could make the right choice regarding which one to buy.

Upon review of all three models, you learned that the Maker is the most powerful among them, but might also be unnecessary unless you were to take your craft to a commercial level. You learned that, similar to Maker, the Explore Air 2 can cut, write, and draw, but not engrave. You learned that this machine may be the best choice for an amateur artist as it works with both sturdy and soft materials, can use a variety of different pens, foils, and iron-on, and pretty much leaves you with very few limitations.

After that, you also learned the advantages of the Cricut Joy. This model isn't only the most affordable. It is also the most convenient and space-efficient. You learned that the Cricut Joy can cut, write, and draw just as well as the others, but it can't work with a lot of sturdy materials, and it can also cut only small sheet dimensions.

Upon learning the pros and cons of each model, the choice you made may have been a bit clearer. It was obvious that you wouldn't lose a lot of the functionality if you chose the Joy, but the creative possibilities of the Maker are simply hard to resist!

Now that you were closer to choosing which Cricut to get, it was time for you to learn how to work in Design Space. This book gave you model-specific lessons covering the use of Design Space depending on the possibility of a specific Cricut. While the software works quite similarly for all Cricuts, knowing which functions and options to access with your model should have made it somewhat easier for you to start making your first projects. You learned how to load images into the software, how to change and adjust them, how to create and add lines and quotes, and more importantly, you learned how to set up the pivotal material options for best results. You learned which steps to take to achieve what you want, which should serve you well once you start working on your own designs.

Upon learning how to work with Cricut, you learned how to care for your die-cutting machine and that regular maintenance is important as your Cricut can collect dust and also build up a residue of materials and scraps with long-term use. You learned that the best way to keep your machine functioning well is to simply clean it regularly with a damp cloth and check its interior to see if there's any adhesive that picked up paper and vinyl scraps. These simple actions can make your Cricut last very long and cut precise and sharp for months before its blade needs a replacement. You also learned which steps to take if your machine doesn't operate properly, as well as how to lubricate it for clean, precise cuts and writing.

After that, you learned what complex operations you can do with each of the models and how each works in terms of cutting, writing, and drawing, as well as which steps are required from you to perform these operations safely. You learned that different Cricuts usually have a larger or fewer number of options to choose from, but that doesn't lessen their value.

You also learned a clear pathway to creating with Cricut, which is to upload an image to your Canvas, make the necessary adjustments, select the operation you wish the Cricut to do (whether to print, cut, or draw, or print-then-cut/draw), load the material, and let the machine do the rest. However, you also learned that the quality and beauty of your creation will depend on the design and material choice, and even small things like choosing the right pen can make a difference in the outcome. For that reason, as you learned, it is important to test out your pens, markers, blades, and materials before you start making a project. That way, you'll know what to expect, and there will be no unpleasant surprises.

This book also gave you a brief overview of the materials that you can use with each Cricut. You learned that not all of them can cut wood, fabric, or leather, but they can work with sufficient numbers of papers and foils for you to create anything you want. From chipboard workstations to personalized mugs, pillows, and even planner stickers, each of the Cricuts work with nice papers for writing cards, cardstock, and chipboards for sturdier designs, like decorations.

Hopefully, you saw that there's a good substitute for each material that you can turn to if your Cricut doesn't support it. You also learned how important it is to use the right materials and mats for your machine. You learned that everything, from material thickness, dimensions, and the finish, affects the work of the machine's blade and the final outcome.

Once you learned everything you needed to operate a Cricut, the time came to start making beginner and intermediate projects. I truly hope that you enjoyed working on these projects and that you found them useful and practicable. You learned how to make a burlap wreath, corsages, stamps, basswood quotes, and personalized beddings and linens. As you found out, there are multiple options in case your Cricut doesn't support the necessary materials, so not having the right machine doesn't mean you have to entirely give up on the project.

If you started practicing, you were probably quick to learn how to work with Design Space, load materials into the machine, handle cut-outs, and more. This gave you the basic skills for Cricut arts and hobbies, but your ambition didn't end there, did it?

Soon, you wanted to learn how to make more advanced projects, so I showed you how to create layered and 3D effects using cutting and engraving on multiple materials. Hopefully, you learned how fun and easy it is to make seemingly difficult projects, and I hope you gave it or will give it a shot.

You learned how to make an intricate shadowbox, how to engrave jewelry, and then how to engrave shadowboxes. You learned how to use layering to make wonderful 3D decorations, as well as how to make nice-looking layered stickers that you can enjoy in your home or commercialize.

Then the time came for you to learn how to create your business with Cricut. As you learned, it is entirely possible for you to make marketable products with Cricut. There's nothing too difficult about it; it only takes time and careful planning to be done in an economically sensible way. You learned that the most difficult thing about keeping your Cricut business profitable is making sure to choose the right materials, designs, and prices. You learned how important it is to price your product correctly, or else you might end up at a financial loss.

Finally, you learned a couple of special tips and tricks when using the Cricut. You learned how to store supplies, how to organize your workspace, and how to make writing and cutting easier and more fun.

I want to leave you with a final note to think carefully about the type of machine you want to purchase. The colorful materials and the prospect of making pretty much anything your heart desires might push you too far, so don't let that happen! Allow your creativity to flow, see which types of products excite you the most, and try to figure out which machine is the best one to use for you to create what you're passionate about.

If this book left you feeling happy, inspired, confident, and smart, kindly leave us an honest review!

References

Sund, A. (2010). Cricut Maker User Manual for Beginners: 2020 User Guide to Master Cricut Maker, Design Space, and Projects: Tools, Set Up Procedures Advance Trick, Tips, and Troubleshooting Hacks Paperback, n.a.

Peterson, C. (2019). Beginner's Guide to Cricut Explore Air 2: A Complete Practical DIY Guide to Master your Cricut Explore Air 2, Cricut Design Space, and Craft Out Creative Cricut Project Ideas (Tips and Tricks) Paperback. n.a.

Yukird, J., Soum, V., Kwon, O. S., Shin, K., Chailapakul, O., & Rodthongkum, N. (2020). 3D paper-based microfluidic device: a novel dual-detection platform of bisphenol A. *Analyst*, 145(4), 1491-1498.

Made in the USA
Monee, IL
10 May 2021